TOTAL
HEALTH CLUB
MANAGEMENT

By Steve Main

Published by

HEALTH
CLUB
MANAGERS

www.HealthClubManagers.com

$19.95
ISBN 978-1-59975-950-0

Table of Contents

Foreword

It is my hope that this book will greatly benefit you as well as the staff that you work with. What I have written here details leadership, sales, and customer-centered approaches which will improve your own work output and positively affect the bottom line of your business.

I borrowed $79,000 in 1994 and started a health club in Carson City, Nevada. I used $20,000 of the $79,000 to start the business—and within a year the entire loan amount was paid back. The one small club I began grew into a multi-club, multi-million dollar business.

Who Will Benefit From This Book

I believe the knowledge and experience shared in this book will benefit anyone working in the fitness industry! Owners can gain an experienced perspective on the industry. General managers can gain insight and improve their management and leadership skills. And staff members of all stripes will be able to read and sharpen their skills, gaining vital tools that will allow them to move into management positions and grow in the industry.

The book is divided into three sections. The first section, *Leading with Excellence,* is ideal for owners, general managers, and anyone seeking to improve their leadership within their organization. Everything in an organization is affected by leadership, and if you improve your leadership, not only will you reach your goals but the people working under you will reach their own goals as well!

The second section, *Successful Sales,* is perfect for anyone working in sales, currently training to be a sales representative, or someone who manages a team of sales reps. This section contains helpful ideas, training tips, and strategies to increase your sales in the fitness industry.

The third section, *Keeping and Growing Your Customer Base,* has several chapters to help you think strategically as you offer customer service to your existing customers and increase the depth and breadth of your customer base in the communities you serve.

All three sections combined come together to form significant part of the fitness club industry and it is my hope that whether you own a chain of clubs or are on your first week of the job, you will be challenged and positively impacted by this book.

TOTAL
HEALTH CLUB
MANAGEMENT

By Steve Main

SECTION ONE:

LEADING WITH EXCELLENCE

Chapter 1:
The Power of Leadership

Leadership is a key ingredient in any organization. Just because someone is an effective leader doesn't mean they are a great leader or even a good leader. What is a leader? What is a great leader? What makes others want to follow a leader? Why would someone want to be a leader? From my experience everything positive in a business organization flows from a leader worth following.

Accomplish Tasks, Obtain Objectives and Reach Goals

Leadership is a key ingredient in any organization. There are many elaborate definitions of leadership, but I will simply define a leader as someone that others follow. However, just being a leader with a lot of followers will not make someone effective in business. An effective business leader influences the actions and behaviors of others in order to *accomplish tasks, obtain objectives* and *reach goals* as a group and as individuals.

A star quarterback in high school who dates the prom queen is admired by his peers. If this same young man decides he is going to cut off one of his pant legs, wear purple socks and two different shoes every day, it won't be long before a hundred of his classmates are doing the same thing. We have all seen examples of people following strange and even immoral behavior. This very effective leader might also drink shots of vodka right after first period. The same pattern occurs with his peers. This very effective leader is not a quality leader in my eyes.

Thought of cloning yourself?

For several years I was one of the owners of a chain of health clubs. We started with one club. It was very easy for me to make sure that everything was done the way I would do it because I was there. We soon opened two more clubs – and suddenly I couldn't be in three places at the same time! That is when the trouble began. I delegated certain tasks to managers in each club, but as you might guess, the tasks didn't get done. Not only did I want the tasks to get done, I wanted them to get done the way I thought they should be done! I delegated the same tasks over and over and explained how I wanted them done. It still wasn't happening. After about 20 times of delegating the same tasks with no results, I would get mad and want to throw stuff! I wanted members to be treated the way I thought they should be treated and I wanted them to get the service they expected. *It wasn't working.* I needed to become an effective leader and I wanted to be a great leader so I could lead people in what needed to be done in my business. This is a good reason for someone to want to be a leader. Our business supports a lot of families and the community very nicely. I think this is a good thing.

I am well respected by all those involved in my business and by most people in the community that interact with me. This may sound arrogant, but I don't think I have the wool pulled over my eyes in assuming this. I have at least become a good leader because the results speak for themselves. We increased our revenue about tenfold in multiple clubs. We started our business by borrowing $79,000 in October 1994. We used about $20,000 and kept the rest in reserve. We repaid all of the $79,000 plus interest before the end of 1995. We built our business into a multi million-dollar business. I didn't do this alone – I was a leader of an amazing group of people – but I learned a lot in the process of building a successful business and consider it a privilege to serve the employees and our community in the ways that I did.

R-E-S-P-E-C-T

Leaders worth following earn respect. Respect must be earned – it isn't just given to you because you are in a *position* of leadership. The following is a list of some of the characteristics and behaviors that earn respect:

- Be open and honest.

Always be open and honest. If you always share both sides of the issues in as much detail as possible, you will build trust. The more information people have the more secure they will feel because you aren't hiding anything from them. People respect the truth and will now trust the information given to them in the future. Winston Churchill led the country of England through many difficult times during World War II. In the darkest of times, no matter how bleak the situation, Churchill was honest with the people he led, knowing that his country would cease following his leadership if he ever misled them.

- Practice what you preach.

A leader must practice what he or she preaches. No one respects a person that says one thing and does another! If you expect employees to be on time, you better be on time. Employees *won't say anything* to me if I'm late for appointments with them because I'm the boss, but if I get on them for being late for one appointment with me when I have been late for two appointments with them they certainly *won't respect me.* If a person always does what he or she says he or she will do, that person earns respect. A person has given their word if they say they are going to be somewhere at a certain time. If you're not sure you can do it, don't say you will. People respect that. Take a promise very seriously. *A promise should be a fact.*

- Take responsibility for actions.

Don't make excuses. Take responsibility for your obligations. The facts are the facts. If you strike out because the umpire made a bad call, it still looks the same in the scorebook. Just admit you struck out. The pitch might have been two feet outside. It wasn't your fault you struck out, but you don't get a do-over. You can't "restart." You are still responsible. I have had employees put the radio on a station that we don't allow and is offensive to our members. That is not *my fault,* but it is *my responsibility.* I need to apologize and make it right. The employee in this case can be written up, suspended or terminated for doing something he or she was instructed not to do. Fault and responsibility are two different things. Never say *it's not my fault.* That is the last thing a customer or employee wants to hear. Take responsibility. People respect that. Apologize when you are wrong or you have failed in your responsibility. In fact, think of it this way: tell people when you are wrong, but never tell them when you are right!

- Don't ask others for more than you'd do yourself.

Never ask someone to do something you are not willing to do, or haven't done yourself. Managers that do this give their staffs the impression that they are better then others. If you take your turn cleaning the toilet in an emergency situation, your staff won't be resentful when you ask them to do it. Always do *more* than what you are asking others to do. You will be respected.

I have learned to do many things that earn respect. It has not been easy for me in many areas, but over the years I continually strive to improve.

What makes people want to follow?

If you are a manager of a club location or a general manager, your staff will follow you because they have to. But how do you lead in such a way that *they want to follow you?* What makes someone want to follow a leader? Let's start with the high school example I gave earlier: if Charlie follows Jerry's example by cutting off one of his pant legs, wearing purple socks and two different shoes, he might be able to date the prom queen's sister!

- Paint a vision

I had to paint a vision of where others want to go. Most people that begin working want to have a successful career *according to their definition.* I knew if I painted the vision to enough people, it would line up with a lot of their definitions of a successful career. The people that buy the vision are ones you want to lead. The people that don't buy into the vision *cannot be led* in the direction you want to go. Painting the vision came easy to me. I painted a vision of wealth sharing, ownership, a future and retirement. I also laid out a plan for the vision. Staff members would not only work for their paycheck today, but also their future. Employees would have to prove themselves first and earn the right to take part in the rewards of the vision. The way an employee does this is by working in the company for a set number of years. That person must also demonstrate their ability to follow my lead in detail, the way I have laid it out in order to accomplish our goals and objectives.

I have created trust and respect with those I work with, so when I tell them they will get the rewards of the vision they believe me. Since the time I first painted the vision, we opened multiple clubs. We started a construction company, a cleaning company, a supply company, a t-shirt company, and multiple consulting companies.

Many former employees have said I don't hold up my end of the bargain. That is true in their cases—because they didn't hold up their end of the bargain! It must be a two-way street. The team of people I work with know without a doubt that I hold up my end of the bargain.

Sharing the wealth

Our Regional Director quit his job as a manager of a large hotel in 1997 and came to work for us. He liked the vision and got excited about it. I was honest about where we were at the time. He worked for peanuts for about six months and put up with our growing pains. It took us years to find our footing and develop a system that worked while I was learning how to better lead. He never took his eyes off the vision or the plan. Now he owns part of three businesses and a fourth that sold for $500,000 that we owned and built up over about a one year period. He also owns part of two different consulting companies, the t-shirt company, the supply company and we're still going strong.

Additionally, twelve of our employees own stock in the cleaning company. This company profited close to $20,000 during its first year. It now owns stock in other companies. In the future, this company may even buy rental properties and continue investing in other ways.

We have multiple employees that have ownership in multiple businesses. The vision is easy to sell now and it is easy for me to lead. I am leading the leaders at this point. The leaders follow my lead. I wanted to be a leader so I could make the business run efficiently. Others follow my lead because they want to grow in their careers. Out of this blend, we have built a team of good leaders that have demonstrated a system that works.

Don't throw things (literally or figuratively!)

- Build a stable management system and structure.

I was able to become a leader and begin leading only after we built a management system and structure. This gave me the vehicle needed to organize a group that could be lead. I might not be a great leader yet, but I am a good leader and working on getting better.

In my experiences, I have made an interesting observation: if I walk into the corporate office, pick up a pen from the office managers desk and throw it at the Regional Director, within 45 minutes, half of our General Managers will be throwing things in their clubs and membership counselors will be rude to members. This is a giant responsibility and I take it very seriously. Being a leader has taught me a lot. The first thing is this: *don't throw things.* This includes the physical act of aggression but also the less subtle ways of power-tripping. A leader not only has responsibility, but also authority and power. I believe a leader should approach his or her responsibility with some fear. If I am cheerful, confident and excited, all those things will trickle down. If I am angry and intense, then displays of anger will trickle down. In larger organizations, leadership trickles down even to people that are not known by the leader!

- Build trust through follow through and consistent ethical behavior.

Discipline is a beneficial characteristic of an effective business leader. A leader must have discipline to follow through on his or her commitments so followers will duplicate this behavior. I cannot emphasize enough to always do what you say. If you are not going to do what you said, don't say it. If you say it, make sure it happens. Remember, followers follow the lead of the leader. Always doing what is said builds trust among followers. Followers should be able to take your words to the bank. Followers know what to expect when the leader always does what is said.

Consistent ethical behavior also builds trust among followers. Followers might not have the same set of ethics but they will know what to expect and what is expected of them. This gives followers a sense of security and will help prevent rumors from circulating. The consistency is a very important key. Without consistency, followers will not know what to expect and insecurity will increase. People feel comfortable when they know what to expect—and that comfort will spread to the corporate environment.

Questions for thought and reflection:

Are you a leader worth following? Why or why not?

Rate yourself in the four characteristics of earning respect. Which is your strongest area? Your weakest? What specific things can you do to continue capitalizing on your strengths? To grow in your weak areas?

- Be open and honest.
- Practice what you preach.
- Take responsibility for actions.
- Don't ask others for more than you'd do yourself.

Notes:

_____

_____

_____

_____

_____

_____

_____

_____

_____

_____

_____

_____

Chapter 2:
Setting Goals

A goal without a plan is just a dream. A goal that is not obtainable is impossible. And a goal that is too easy is not a worthy goal to begin with!

To be an effective leader of others (and yourself), you must set realistic but challenging goals. Striving for a goal is a way to measure success. The higher the goal, the greater the accomplishment is. Conversely, if you never set goals then you will never have a basis for evaluation. (If you never create a target, you will never hit it!) Goals are a part of our health club business *every hour of every day*.

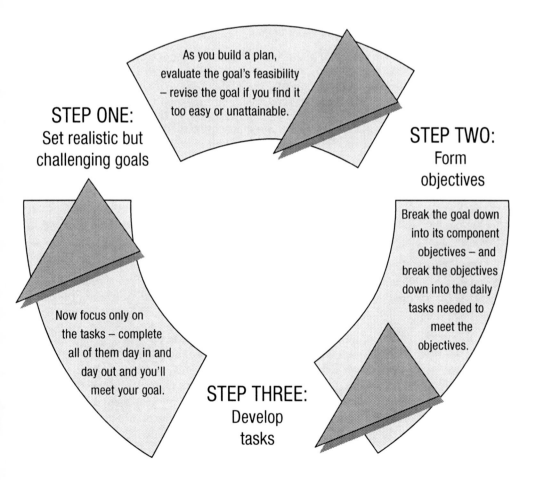

STEP ONE:
Set realistic but challenging goals

As you build a plan, evaluate the goal's feasibility – revise the goal if you find it too easy or unattainable.

STEP TWO:
Form objectives

Break the goal down into its component objectives – and break the objectives down into the daily tasks needed to meet the objectives.

STEP THREE:
Develop tasks

Now focus only on the tasks – complete all of them day in and day out and you'll meet your goal.

Step One: Set the goal. Setting the goal is the first step—a plan must be developed to reach the goal. Once we start to build the plan, the goal sometimes becomes ridiculous. The plan exposes the feasibility of the goal. We might find that the goal is impossible or that it is too easy.

Step Two: Form Objectives. The next step after setting the goal is to form objectives. If the objectives are met, the goal will be obtained. Tasks must be developed in order to meet the objectives. If your goal is challenging, then chances are that it may be overwhelming to you at times, and sometimes viewed by others as impossible.

Take, for example, long-distance races such as marathons or triathlons. Runners may set goals to run in certain races, either to compete or simply to finish. To fitness buffs, a 5K or 10K run seems understandable and fairly easy if you are in decent shape. The harder you train, the more feasible a half-marathon or marathon becomes. But once you train for races over 15 or 20 miles in length you must *form objectives* that need to be met as you train. These might be certain distances or certain times that you set as objectives on a monthly basis as you head toward race day. Otherwise the 26.2 miles would seem overwhelming and you would be tempted to quit.

To those who do not run, 26.2 miles seems impossible. But experienced runners understand more than just the goal. They understand the objectives which must be reached every few weeks or every month that will enable them to reach the final goal, to finish their race.

A triathlon is another great example of forming objectives. If your goal is to complete an Olympic-length triathlon (roughly broken down as a one-mile swim, a twenty-five-mile bike and a six-mile run), you must form objectives or you will be overwhelmed trying to alternate between 3 disciplines and be tempted to quit. Remember this: to an outsider, your goal might seem impossible. People who do not work out might think triathletes are crazy! But if you've evaluated your goal and it is challenging and realistic, then be sure to break your goal down into objectives so that you can hammer away at those on your way to reach the ultimate goal, whatever that is for you.

Step Three: Developing the Tasks. Tasks are different from goals or objectives because tasks are performed daily. Tasks are *daily requirements*. If the tasks cannot be done, the goal is impossible. Remember this: if the tasks are too few or too easy, the goal is also too easy.

Once the tasks are set, all the focus should be taken off the goal and put on the tasks. It transfers some of the fear and anxiety we might feel about the goal and creates immediacy: today I can decide whether I will hit my goal or not, based on whether or not I complete the tasks I've set out for today. How badly do I want this? The people that have the discipline to complete all the tasks day in and day out will hit their goal. And if you get lazy or lose your discipline for a few days, then you are in jeopardy of missing the goal!

If you hire a new sales representative, it is critical to help them set her or his goals. First, ask how much money she wants to make. Then lay out goals, objectives—and, most importantly, tasks.

Example:

Goal: $3,000 per month for a new sales rep

The rep is paid two times a month and needs to make $1,500 each paycheck.
Objective 1: Make $1,500 per check. ($1,100 commission per check plus base pay)
Objective 2: Write $3,000 in new dues memberships per pay-period.
Objective 3: Write $2,000 in new paid-in-full memberships per pay-period.
Objective 4: Work six days per week, writing 2 new dues memberships per day and a
       paid-in-full membership every third day.
Objective 5: Give a tour to a walk-in guest. (In order to tour a walk-in, the rep should
have satisfied a requirement, which might include either 15 new memberships for the
month or having sold a membership the day before.)

Now, create a checklist your representative can perform daily to achieve these objectives.

The best way to create tasks is through a **checklist system.** A checklist is a list of
tasks which must be completed hour-by-hour. These tasks are not goals or objectives but
rather the required component parts of those objectives which will move you toward your
goal. Tasks are set up in such a way that any person who has the discipline and skill to
accomplish the right tasks day in and day out will meet their objectives and accomplish
their goal.

Of course, discipline is the big key to success. Most people don't have it! All the skill
in the world is useless without discipline when it come to obtaining a challenging goal. The
discipline to stay on the road map of success requires *relentless focus* on the tasks that
must be completed in a consistent manner. Remember, any person who does not
accomplish their required tasks for just one day is in danger of missing their goal.

When the tasks don't work: It is possible for someone to complete the checklist
completely every day and not reach the goal. If this happens, you need to adjust the tasks
so your road map toward the goal is accurate. Many times the tasks on the checklist must
be changed or modified. For example, the person performing the tasks might not have the
skill to perform the tasks at the required level. If I do everything a professional singer does
in the same manner the professional did to reach the same accomplishment, it won't work.
I can't sing! I don't have the ability to perform the tasks at the needed skill level.

If you complete your checklist every day, with the right tasks performed at a high skill
level, and allow enough time for the tasks to have an impact, you will obtain your goal
in the timeframe you set.

Your Turn

We do not always obtain our leadership and management goals. But if you pursue your tasks, objectives and goals with passion and discipline, you will get close or reach your goals much of the time. Take time right now to write down two or three goals that you have in your current business.

GOAL 1   GOAL 2   GOAL 3

Objective 1   Objective 1   Objective 1

Objective 2   Objective 2   Objective 2

Objective 3   Objective 3   Objective 3

Daily Required Tasks   Daily Required Tasks   Daily Required Tasks

Notes:

_____

_____

_____

_____

_____

_____

_____

_____

_____

_____

_____

_____

_____

_____

_____

_____

_____

_____

_____

_____

_____

_____

_____

_____

_____

Chapter 3:
Defining Your Price Structure

Setting the prices for your health club services can make or break your business! It can have a significant effect on the amount of profit (or loss!) every month and every year. But making a mistake on setting the price for your memberships and services can cost you *more* then your business. It can cost you your home and everything in your bank accounts. Price setting in the health club industry is more of an art than a science. Although you may not be able to set the perfect price, there are principles you can apply to keep your business from losing money.

Price Theory One: Create Volume

I'd like to discuss some of the general advantages and disadvantages of the low price theory. (We will leave out enrollments and processing fees for now.) Since there are so many variables, let's keep it simple by assuming there is no competition in your town of 25,000 people. You have a 15,000 square foot facility with ample cardio stations, plenty of weight training equipment and a good group-fitness program. If your club offers dues memberships at $19 a month or lower, you will maximize your memberships. If you are a good operator and have a good sales staff you can expect to have 2,500 members. We have at least 10% of the population as members of our clubs in all of our locations. (Our prices are twice this and we have competition.) In the scenario I have laid out, you should have 2,500 members without any problems.

Advantages:

- When people pay less, they are less likely to cancel their membership.

- People will go lengthy periods without using the club but keep their memberships.

- You have maximized your membership base so you will have more people using the club on a daily basis then you would if your rates were double.

- With more people using the club, you will sell more drinks, nutrition bars, supplements and apparel.

- Since the membership fees are low, your members will also have more money to spend in your facility. They will justify spending money in your club because they have such a low monthly fee.

- Low rates help to deter competition if you have a nice facility.

- The higher the usage in your club will make it easier to sell memberships because there is more energy. Most people like to go to popular places.

- The low rate theory works very well if the club is of good size, has 100 pieces of cardio or more, has plenty of parking, has very little debt, is in a densely populated area and has fairly low overhead.

Disadvantages:

- The lower your monthly dues, the more of your dues payments will be rejected because of insufficient funds. Some people figure they can afford the low dues, but are in actuality financially irresponsible and live above their means. If you have a member with a checking account balance of $0.00, it doesn't matter if the payment is $79 or $1. It will be rejected.

- You must sell twice as many memberships as a club that charges double your rate.

- The majority of the population will not come into a health club even if it is free. Many won't come in even if you pay them. The percentage of people using health clubs in the United States is increasing, but you might not be able to significantly increase that percentage with low rates. The maximum percentage for people using a health club is probably about 15% depending on the geographic region you live in.

- There is a point of no return. You will have just as many members at $7 a month as you will at $9 a month.

- Increased traffic flow increases wear and tear in your club. It is more costly to keep the club clean; equipment breaks down more often, and the club goes through more supplies.

- The club might use up the parking you have which makes it difficult to sell memberships. If a person is coming to shop your club and can't find parking, they will leave. If a member consistently has trouble finding parking, they will cancel. Their membership is useless.

Many advocate selling very low priced or discounted memberships to obtain volume. Others advocate high prices and creating value. Anyone who says one way or the other is always better is not an expert, because one size does not fit all.

Price Theory Two: Create Value

Most of the pros and cons for the higher priced theory are opposite of the lower priced theory. Let's use the same scenario we used for the low priced theory. The higher priced theory *emphasizes value and results.* In this case, the club doesn't just want the members' money and hope they use the club less. They want the members to use the club and get results. An individual will pay a lot more and be happy if they lose 50 pounds. That person is also a walking billboard! The member wants to pay more and get more. They want a training program set up for them and they want follow-up from a professional trainer. They want any questions they have answered in a professional manner. They want a very clean facility. These members will not leave if they get the service and results they are looking for. These members won't slam your weight stacks or dumbbells. They won't spit on the floor, put holes in the wall, throw toilet paper on the floor or urinate in the sauna. (These things will probably happen with some of the low paying members!) The higher paying member is a different breed. They will take pride in the club like it is their own. When you debit their account for dues, the money will be there. They will pay as much as $79 to $89 for the same 15,000 square foot facility in this scenario.

Advantages:

- You will have less expense with the higher paying memberships due to less wear and tear, less traffic flow and less administrative costs.

- The club can make a nice profit with far fewer members. The club only has to sell one membership for every 2 or 3 sold at the lower priced clubs.

- The club can run with a leaner, more professional sales staff.

- Members have more money and will spend more on higher priced items or services such as personal training or massage.

Disadvantages:

- Higher paying members are much harder to please. They can be very demanding and quite unreasonable at times. Make one mistake and they are gone.

- They are much quicker then the low paying member to cancel their membership. If they don't use the club for a period of time, they will cancel.

- The higher your prices, the higher your cancellation percentage will be. You will have fewer cancellations than the low priced club because you have fewer members and you take care of them, but the members you have will be harder to keep.

- Higher priced clubs have shrunk their market. There are less potential members the higher the price goes.

- The high priced club that reaches a respectable level of success is inviting competition. If your club sells memberships at a high price and your community is growing, the competition will come.

There are far too many variables to say one way is better than the other. Every club has different variables. The following are some of the factors:

1. How big is your club?
2. What is your cash reserve?
3. How much cardio equipment do you have in your club?
4. How much cardio equipment can you add in your club?
5. How many competitors do you have in your area?
6. How big are your competitors' clubs?
7. How much cardio equipment do your competitors have?
8. What is your overhead?
9. Is your equipment paid off?
10. Are you in a city or rural area?
11. What are the demographics of your area?
12. How many people live within a 3-mile radius?
13. How many people live within a 5-mile radius?
14. What is the median household income?
15. Do you have multiple clubs in the area?

16. Do any of your competitors have multiple clubs in the area?
17. What are your competitors' prices and what do they offer?
18. What is your dues base?
19. How much of the market have you captured?
20. What is the growth rate of your area?
21. Is your market open for new potential competitors?
22. Is there a vacuum in your area?
23. Have you created a vacuum?
24. Have your competitors created a vacuum?
25. Do people in your community commute to work?
26. What is the traffic flow like?
27. Does the average person in your community drive long distances on a regular basis?
28. If you have multiple locations in adjacent towns, do people commute from one town to another?
29. Do you have competitors that have multiple locations in adjacent towns?
30. Do your competitors have aggressive sales staffs?

More Art Than Science

These are just some of the factors that must be considered when you set your pricing. You must also try to look into the future and predict it the best you can. As you can see, it would be stupid for me or anyone else to say, "This is what your pricing should be" or "This is the best way."

It is not hard to figure out that a club selling dues memberships for $10 a month will have more members than a similar club that sells memberships for $100 a month. Will the club with more members make more money? The answer is *maybe*. What is hard to figure out is which club will have more members if one sells memberships for $30 a month and the other sells memberships for $35 a month. The same club might have just as many members if they sell memberships for $35 a month as opposed to $30 a month. If that same club offers memberships at $20 a month and has 2,000 members, is that better than 1,000 members at $35 a month? Again, the answer is *maybe*. If your club is the only club in town, you will probably have just as many members at $35 a month as you would at $30 a month. But have you left the door open, or created a vacuum for another operator with deep pockets to come into your town with a little nicer club and more equipment that will charge $30 a month? Yet again, the answer is *maybe*. That is where all the variables come in. This is not an exact science. It is an art, a battle of nerves. It is a brain game! *You are competing even if you don't have competition.* And you must not just look at the present, but into the future as well.

Will People Rush to Your Club?

I'd like to make an important point at this time on something I have gained from my many years of experience in the health club industry. This point will ease your fears if you operate a club and prevent you from *making a disastrous mistake* if you plan on opening a club.

Many people that are new to this business think they can open a club in a community and *take half of the members* from existing and established clubs because they are run poorly, their price is too high, they are dirty, have bad equipment or bad service. **Do not count on this.** I will say it again: do not plan a new club with this as a strategy. Any members you gain from other facilities will usually only be a trickle on a percentage basis. This strategy is a big gamble and is not a good reason to choose a location. *It doesn't matter what the competition's price structure is or how it is run.* A number of years ago I spoke with a very nice older woman that came into one of our clubs because the club she was at had just closed. The club she left was as run down as it gets! With tears in her eyes she explained to me that she was very happy to join our club and she thought it was very nice. The problem was that she was going to miss her friend terribly. They met every morning and exercised together. Her friend joined one of our other locations because it was closer to her home. I really felt for this lady so I said, "Why don't you use our other club also?" She said, "It's too far. What if it snows?" Members in a health club bond much more with each other then they do with your location. People also like their old sweat shirts or shoes! How often have you seen people that wear something until it practically falls off of them? In the case of this nice lady, her club got bulldozed! If it didn't, she never would have left.

People don't like change. Having learned that lesson, we have incorporated a Member Wall at our locations, with pictures of some of our members with a short blurb of information and a hobby they might have. This helps get members bonding with each other. Unless a new club takes all of our members, they will not profit on the business we have built. Even if it was possible for a new club to take all of an existing club's members, they can never take the old shoe.

Case Study

We started pre-sales for the first club we built in November of 1994. After extensive research we chose our location. The town had about 45,000 people in it. I knew about 10% of the population would join a club, and there were 3 existing clubs in the town. I knew from shopping these clubs (and talking to staff members or operators that definitely talked too much!) that one club at the opposite end of town had about 900 members. Another club in the middle of town had about 600 members. The third club made the very unwise choice of charging people $2 a day and had no members to speak of. (Why would anyone commit if they could pay $2 whenever they felt like going to the gym?) The first 2 clubs were selling dues memberships in the mid thirty-dollar range.

As you know, 10% of 45,000 is 4,500. I knew there was a market in this town of at least 3,000 potential members. We started our pre-sale memberships with a $79 processing fee and $22 a month. Our goal was 2,000 members by the end of our first year in business. We had 2,000 members after pre-sales. We reached our goal before we even opened the club in February of 1995! We took very few members from the existing clubs—if we had counted on that for our membership base, we would have failed! Our members came from the 3,000 potential members that were not yet members of another club.

Watch that Fuzzy Feeling

If you are a current owner of a health club, let me warn you before your warm fuzzy feeling gets too warm. All three of those clubs that existed when we came into the market are now gone. Many more have come and gone in our market. Competition can and will hurt your profit—I didn't say it couldn't. I said an existing club would lose very few members to a new club. When a new club comes into your market, *the competition is for new business.* If your club writes $30,000 a month in new memberships, it will decrease, no matter how great you are. The new club *will* get some of that new business. It is now a matter of the better operator fighting for the lion's share. If your profit was $15,000 a month and the new club gets $20,000 of your new business, you're in trouble.

The first club we opened averaged about $30,000 in new business until we opened another larger club on the other side of town. That new club averaged about $25,000 to $30,000 in new memberships and our old club averaged about $20,000 in new memberships. This was a calculated risk, but it paid off for us because we increased the total new sales in our town. We also were able to cut our overhead by spreading it out into multiple clubs. When new clubs came into our market, our dues cancellations did not change! If anything, our cancellations had become fewer.

The Dues Base

The biggest strength of a health club is its dues base. The key is striking the balance between dues memberships and paid-in-full (PIF) memberships. Your pricing and sales structure must be set in order to build a strong dues base. We tried to keep our dues to PIF ratio at 7 to 3. (That is 7 dues memberships for every 3 PIF's.) There are advantages and disadvantages to each type of membership just like there are for high and low memberships. Our dues memberships are a one-year commitment. We charge an enrollment fee and a processing fee. (Part or all of the entire enrollment may be waived depending on if the buyer has a gift certificate or coupon.) Usually a discount is given for a PIF membership for one year. Enrollment and processing may be waived or extra months may be added onto the membership. If enrollment and processing is waived, multiply the monthly dues by 12 months.

These are some of the advantages to the PIF membership:

1. The club saves money on the billing, administrative and collecting process.
2. A lower commission percentage is paid on a PIF as apposed to a dues membership.
3. A PIF increases cash flow for the month it is received.
4. A PIF increases the profit margin for the month it is received.
5. The money is in the bank. There are no dues payments to be rejected.

These are some of the advantages to the dues membership:

1. Dues memberships increase the club's residual income or monthly receivables.
2. Dues memberships build financial security.
3. A potential member can get a membership started for less money.
4. Dues memberships help to establish an accurate budget.

The key to building a strong health club business is the dues base. Residual monthly income can be counted on to help make decisions on future expenditures or expansions. Selling the right combination of dues and PIF memberships maximizes profit. It should be realized that a PIF membership should also be residual income on a yearly basis. If the member is serviced well and motivated, that member will rejoin every year. If the dues memberships get too high on a monthly percentage, the immediate monthly profit shrinks. If the percentage of monthly PIF memberships gets too high, future profits shrink.

Mastering the Art of Pricing

If I had the only club in a town of 25,000 people, I would definitely try to capture more of the market by keeping the rates reasonable. If I had a club or was planning on building a club in an area that has competitors that use the low priced theory, with a lot of cardio equipment and parking, I would use the high priced theory. I would build a smaller club and emphasize service, quality and results. I would market the people that are looking for something other than a zoo with hard bodies. Remember this: the majority of people (up to 90%) are not members of a health club *but should be.* A smaller club that emphasizes results, value and service is what most people need.

Setting prices for your health club is not the only factor that will determine the success or failure of the club, but it is certainly one of the biggest. A club must be marketed and sold effectively. Even if an operator could establish the perfect price, it would be of little benefit if the club is not sold efficiently. The health club business is no different than any other business: all aspects of the business must operate at a high level to maximize profit.

Worksheet

Complete the following worksheet, answering the following questions and analyzing your pricing structure. Where are you at now? Where should you be? Use the following as a guide to help you analyze and potentially alter your current pricing:

How big is your club?

What is your cash reserve?

How much cardio equipment do you have in your club?

How much cardio equipment can you add in your club?

How many competitors do you have in your area?

How big are your competitors' clubs?

How much cardio equipment do your competitors have?

What is your overhead?

Is your equipment paid off?

Are you in a city or rural area?

What are the demographics of your area?

How many people live within a 3-mile radius?

How many people live within a 5-mile radius?

What is the median household income?

Do you have multiple clubs in the area?

Do any of your competitors have multiple clubs in the area?

What are your competitors' prices and what do they offer?

What is your dues base?

How much of the market have you captured?

What is the growth rate of your area?

Is your market open for new potential competitors?

Is there a vacuum in your area?

Have you created a vacuum?

Have your competitors created a vacuum?

Do people in your community commute to work?

What is the traffic flow like?

Does the average person in your community drive long distances on a regular basis?

If you have multiple locations in adjacent towns, do people commute from one town to another?

Do you have competitors that have multiple locations in adjacent towns?

Do your competitors have aggressive sales staffs?

Notes:

SECTION TWO:

SUCCESSFUL SALES

Chapter 4:
The *Why* Factor

Your Club Will Not Sell Itself

Total health club management requires that you have a well-trained, organized and managed sales staff. Everything starts with the sale. If there are no sales, nothing else matters. Without sales, it doesn't matter how clean or friendly your club is. It doesn't matter what your prices are, how big your club is, how good your programs are or how much equipment you have. I am not saying that all the other aspects of your club are not important. I am saying that *selling is the most important.* If all other aspects of your club are perfect but you have no sales, your club will fail. Do not assume your club will sell itself. *You* must sell it.

We trained our sales staff to sell in two different ways. The first way is selling on emotion. This worked great for us when we had just one club and a couple of very natural and extremely intelligent sales reps. Selling on emotion is very difficult, if not impossible, to teach. It is very intuitive. When we expanded to multiple locations, we had to come up with a more systematic approach to selling. But the emotional element, the "why" factor, is present in every sale.

The "Why" Factor

There is a reason that each person shops for a health club membership. That reason is emotional. A potential member will tell you *what* they want in most cases, but they won't tell you *why.* At the end of all the wants lies *the reason.* A young college athlete may want to lift weights. Why? Build strength in his body. Why? Improve his athletic performance. Why? He wants to be first string instead of second string. Why? He wants to gain recognition and accolades from the community. Why? He thinks the girl he is in love with will notice him. That's the "Why" Factor.

I will give you three actual examples of sales I have made using this method. Some sales reps may think this is manipulation. I don't see it that way, because all I am doing is connecting the dots.

Example One: The Ex-Boyfriend

A young girl came into the club very interested in doing group-fitness classes. I analyzed her physical appearance and body language during a quick ten-minute discussion about her. I asked her questions about herself and the status of her life at the time. I am pretty good at getting people to open up. I discovered that her boyfriend broke up with her about a week ago and was now dating someone else. She mentioned this very casually.

It only took me about ten minutes to connect the dots. She did not walk in and proclaim, "I want my boyfriend back." Her initial comment was, "I'm interested in doing group fitness." I concluded that she probably wanted to make her ex-boyfriend jealous. I said, "I don't know what's wrong with your ex-boyfriend, but we're going to set you up on a great program. He's going to be sorry he broke up with you." She couldn't grab the pen out of my hand fast enough to sign the papers. It wasn't until later that she asked about the price. Price is usually not an issue if you figure out the "Why" factor.

Example Two: Too Young to Die

An older woman entered the club inquiring about memberships. I quickly turned the conversation to her. It was brought up in the conversation that her husband had passed away recently. I'm sure she was heartbroken, but what really seemed to bother her the day we spoke was the fear of her *own death.* She didn't walk in, grab someone and say, "I'm too young to die." My comment to her was this: "We're going to set you up on a great program to maximize your health. I hope you don't mind being around for another 40 years." She signed up quickly. Barriers are quickly removed when you figure out the "Why" factor.

Example Three: Dealing with stress

A woman walked in with a couple of young children. Once again, the conversation turned toward her. I quickly found out that her husband was coming home every night and yelling at her and the kids. He had a very stressful job. Imagine this lady walking in and saying, "My husband is mean. Can anyone fix that?" She didn't say that. But I told her that when exercise is done properly, hormones called endorphins are released into the bloodstream, which has a calming effect on a person. I also told her that we have a great kids area. We could watch her children while she and her husband exercised. She quickly signed up the whole family.

We have a number of sales reps in multiple facilities now. As you expand it is not easy to replicate the Why factor but it is always there. Obviously, a business must change and adapt as it grows, and you must equip your sales department with a variety of tools that will increase their paycheck and increase your bottom line. What follows in these chapters are several elements and tools for successful sales.

The Role of the First Impression

Many times, you are selling yourself as much or more than you are selling the product or what it can do for people. The importance of the introduction is critical! First impressions are very, very important. You never get a second chance to get it right.

First, try to build rapport immediately. When a potential member comes into the club, introduce yourself first. Remember, the man or woman who comes in may never have been in a health club before. It might be all new to them, and they may be a little nervous about being there.

If your club has potential members fill out a fitness profile at a front desk, there is a really good chance that right after that they are going to start putting up some of their defenses. You want to be as gentle as you can be. If they say, "I don't want to fill anything out," make sure your staff's first words are, "Okay, that's okay." If your front desk is really confident; they will start the sale for you.

To do well at sales you want to always treat people right. What you are selling is an excellent product, one they very well may buy.

When you go up to them, introduce yourself and tell them, "What I'd like to do is take a minute and go over your fitness profile, and see what you would like to accomplish in terms of fitness. We'll show you the facility and then we'll sit down and go over some membership options to get you started. How does that sound?"

Remember you are building your *yeses*. Try to ask questions where you expect to get the answer "yes." If they say yes to the profile review then start your process. If they say, "I don't have time today," then find out how much time they have and take it from there. If right away they say, "There is no way I am doing it today," you need to start asking questions until you get a yes answer. If they say, "I don't have time today to do all that," ask them how much time he or she does have. "Do you have fifteen minutes? We'll take a quick tour of the facility and we'll go over some membership options." If they say yes then you have a possibility of a sale at that point.

If they are closing the door already to you selling them the membership, then address it by just showing them the facility. So if they say, "We can look at the facility but I'm not going to join today," then try to find out what they are thinking. If they say that they will join the next month, you can discuss a great promotion that you have currently.

Remember that money might be an issue for some people:

"We've got a great promotion going right now. Is it a money issue? If it is a money issue we can work out a payment plan that can work for you."

Whatever you say, try to drive them toward a yes answer. Then you can start the process toward signing a member!

Notes:

Chapter 5:
Growing Your Network

A Successful Start in Sales

If you have never been involved in sales before, there is definitely a learning curve. If you master the curve and get a consistent groove or flow to your work it can be a very lucrative profession. But when you start off you will have to learn the ropes and pay your dues. You will need to be teachable, and you will need to learn how to treat people. I want to encourage you that you can do it! You can learn the confidence so that when you hit those walls and face challenges in sales you can push through, the same way you might lift weights and push through, getting one or two more reps into a set, even when you're exhausted.

If you feel like you are struggling with those phones—either making phone calls or appointments or taking in phone calls—you will eventually learn how to deal with that struggle and overcome it. You have the potential of improvement!

Checklists

Earlier in the book I wrote about the power of goal setting, and how to break goals down into objectives and tasks. Checklists are the master of the task. If you live by the checklist, you will be successful at reaching your goals—because the tasks on the list are *required* to reach the goal!

It is critical for your organization to have checklists top to bottom: counselors should have checklists, cleaners should have checklists, and front desk workers should have checklists. Customer service managers should have checklists to check those checklists and the regional and district managers should have checklists to check *those* checklists! That way, the whole system has accountability and the person on the very top, a general partner, could call the newest counselor in the newest club and ask, *"How did the training go today?"*

"Oh, it went great."

"What did you train on?"

"We trained on buddy referrals."

"What did they show you to do?"

"They popped the DVD in and then we did some role playing."

That is what the person at the top wants to hear. Checklists are powerful tools to manage the tasks which manage the objectives which manage the goals. If you want to reach your goals, make a checklist!

Of course, it is possible to bluff a certain amount if the general partner calls a manager and the manager tells him what he wants to hear and no one has really learned anything. But if that manager is truly accountable for what is learned, and checklists are managed well, goals will be reached and paychecks will get fatter! It is really important to implement tasks through checklists from top to bottom to be consistent and effective as a business.

Starting Your Sales Network.

As you know, your sales network is built by appointments, appointments, appointments. Face to face appointments! Make these appointments from outside the club, inside the club, off your buddy referrals and telephone inquiries. An appointment-based system is essential to successful health club management.

If your club has a lot of advertising, that is great. But advertising has a cost: it makes counselors lazy. Sales reps end up sitting on their backsides and waiting for the gravy. The most cost effective approach instead is giving sales reps a lucrative pay package based on appointments getting done, and taking good enough care of people that their friends want to come in and join. The better care you take of them, the more friends of theirs will join and the more buddy referrals you will receive.

Learn to work the phones! The counselors that make more phone calls work more productive hours. And the longer that you are doing your job, the more productive your phone calls will get. You will end up with more sources, you will have more buddy referrals and you will have better lead boxes out there from which you will receive some of your leads.

Train Your Weakness

If you make one-hundred phone calls and you are making two appointments, that's a weakness! Out of 100 new phone calls, you should be making at least twelve appointments. If you struggle making appointments, that is where you should get additional training.

If you set twelve appointments and no one is showing up, those are what we call *pity appointments,* which are appointments where you are nice enough and persistent enough for someone to make an appointment with you *to get you off the phone*—but they do not show up. If you cannot get any shows, that is where you should get additional training.

I've Got No One to Call. Find someone! Get a lead box out there, find corporate contacts, work the floor for buddy referrals and get out there and make some appointments!

You should have people to call. If you struggle finding people to call, then get additional training so you can make good appointments. And out of twelve appointments, you should have half of them show up.

Always Be Closing! If you have six people show up for appointments and none of those join the club, that is not a very good closing average! About half should join. And out of the three who join you should get about six buddy referrals, as well as referrals from the three who do not join. If you are having trouble getting people to the close, then be sure to get additional training in that area. If you are not closing enough, be sure to get help. And if you have trouble getting buddy referrals, be sure to get additional training in that area also.

Most of what you do should lead to appointments which will bring larger paychecks—and a stream of people who have joined over the years will continue to be big members and bring you other members who will come in and join.

Outside the Club

Is sales easy? No, definitely not. The job is not easy. You are not able to sit there and say, "Hey, all I need to do is get 100 phone calls and I'm going to get rich." That is not the case. As I wrote before, you have to pay your dues. You have to be teachable, and continue to learn, train, and learn how to handle phone calls. You have to learn how to treat the members right, how to be polite, how to talk without becoming angry or defensive, and how to interact outside the clubs.

Try to wear your logo everywhere:

"Oh, you work for that health club?"

"Yes, I do."

That is one way the conversation could go. How about this instead:

"Oh, you work for that health club?"

"Yes, have you ever seen the clubs?"

Do not just say "yes." Instead, seize the opportunity! Do not beat people up or harass them if they are busy working. You can just be polite and ask a simple question: "Have you ever seen the clubs? We just opened a new one." See what they are interested in, get a business card out, and seize those opportunities. You never know who is going to come in and say, "My friend works at the grocery store and she gave me your card and she said to come in and see you." That is not an appointment you made, but it is a contact you made, and you made an impression on somebody and took the time to give your card. Develop your contacts!

Why Rely on an Actor or Model?

There are other clubs and other chains that rely on actors, models or athletes to drive business to their clubs. Their marketing strategies are always focused on having someone else do the work to drive up business. It ultimately engenders laziness in your sales staff. The mentality becomes, "Why isn't the marketing department doing a better job creating foot traffic in here?"

Here is the fundamental problem: in the past few years there has been a massive shift in what works in marketing. People are continually shuffling around what they are willing to pay attention to. I used to find that (a few years ago) time management was the buzzphrase. People were constantly focused on their time and how they can manage it better. But more recently *attention* is the buzzword. People "scan and click" even when they are just reading.

The entire advertising word is going through a crisis of epic proportions, and companies are demanding that marketers figure it out and start creating advertising that works. That might be fine and good, but I prefer to build a company with young, energetic, hard-working people. Some others might count on a model, athlete or actor to build their business—but even if our clubs could have afforded that early on we would not have gone that route. Because if a famous face replaces sales reps connecting with other businesses and doing their jobs, then I want nothing of it. Gift bags are a part of this mix, too. I always want the team using their legs, using their cars to go out and introduce themselves—get things going.

Gift Bag Example

Let's say that you want to do a drawing in your club. To create an incentive for buddy referrals, you offer ten raffle tickets to a member for every five people they refer to the club. The raffle is for something you've developed in your own network. If you know someone who works in a hair salon, you can arrange a set of discounts that you give people in the club. In turn, the hair stylist can utilize discounts that you have for signing up for membership and can send people to you. You can read more about gift bags in Section Three of this book. It is a fantastic way to build a network and create mutually-beneficial foot traffic.

Don't Say It Can't Be Done!

If you bluff your way through the appointment-making process or the buddy-referral checklist it might work for a while, but eventually you will fail. The most important piece of this sales process is to believe that it can be done—because it can. I did it myself for years and it works. Do not try to keep the same appointment three times a week for a month to satisfy your supervisor that you have an "appointment." You can reschedule a time or two, but otherwise that's a dead-end. It would serve you better to make a good, honest effort with five fresh people coming in the club than with an appointment who continually no-shows. *Continually seek new contacts and create new energy!*

Making Lead Boxes Work for You

If you set up a drawing box or lead box, be prepared to talk honestly about what you are giving away. Remember, people are becoming more and more marketing savvy and don't want to hear a bunch of garbage.

Be sure to explain what you are giving them and how they can come in the club and take advantage of it. Meet with the potential member, get her or him a pass, and list out three people he would like to introduce the club to. And don't stop there—if the guest won three passes and only accepts one, keep the other two and work the floor.

> "We had a guest who didn't need a second or third pass for the club. Do you know anyone who could use this?"
>
> *"Yes, I think I do"*
>
> "Well, I only have two, so what I would like to do is call and make sure that they are interested, because I have other members that would love to have these. Can you give me their name and number?"

"Well, I don't want you calling them."

"This is what I will do: I will put your name on it for now and I am going to hold onto it. Give them a call after your workout or come by and see me we will call them together. I want to make sure that these are going to go to people who use them because usually we only give out five day-passes that are good for a month."

Work the two passes until you give them away. And then get another one off of another membership.

Find Your Niche

In sales, try various approaches and figure out what works well for you. Play to your strengths. You will likely find out that one or two methods of building your network just seem to flow easily for you. Great! Capture the energy from these methods and ride the waves of that method. Find what is natural for you.

If there are certain approaches to sales that work less well for you, you might be tempted to ignore them or forget about them altogether. This would be a mistake! Why? Because six months from now you might be training other people in a variety of sales techniques and you will need to have those skills in your arsenal. Do you personally need to utilize every one daily or weekly? Of course not. But you may need to train others using those skills and so you will need to have them at your disposal.

Remember to focus on customer service! If you treat people right, you will have better customer service and you will have more people wanting to have their friends join, because it is good for them and because they will be treated right. Sometimes you won't have to create an incentive for buddy referrals because your product is great: if you have a great club, they will get the results they want and they will want their friends to come in anyway.

Pick Up the Ball

In sales, try your best to create an environment where you have great working relationships with your members. If a sales rep leaves, make sure you do not drop the ball on the leads he or she has developed. Step right in and pick it up.

Introduce yourself to your new contacts and new businesses, and make the transition as smooth as possible. And if there are accounts that you cannot handle well, a new sales rep would be happy to have it. Take a new rep in there with you and set up the introduction:

"Hey this is Mike. He is taking over your account. If there is anything you need, if you need any passes to give to your employees, or if you need more passes to give to your good customers let us know. By the way, we are having a party at the end of the month. Would you like to come and set up a table and put some samples of your food? Maybe we can create some business for you."

Try to do ten things at once! You never know what it is going to lead to.

Notes:

Chapter 6:
Touring a Potential Member

If you are meeting with a walk-in guest or have a scheduled appointment with a contact, make sure you utilize the tools at your disposal, particularly the fitness profile and the tour of the facility. Each of these will help you build rapport with the guest and create a positive sales environment.

Utilize a Fitness Profile

The fitness profile is an extremely helpful tool in increasing sales. Try to bring them over to your desk and tell them you are going to go over basic questions that they already know the answers to. Try to build rapport with the guest.

"What are your goals? What is your time frame?"

These are some basic questions you can ask   But don't stop there. Next, try to find an innate or emotional desire within the profile. Someone might have a goal of losing twenty pounds. Find the "Why" Factor. Don't stop at the twenty-pound goal. There is a reason behind it! Do they have a class reunion coming up? Do they struggle with fatigue? Are they worried about their health? Find the emotional reason that they need to join and work together with them toward their goal.

Sometimes a potential member's weight-loss goals are too unrealistic. If that happens, try to set a realistic goal for them:

"What we'd like to do is take that first step, and address that first twenty pounds. When you lose twenty pounds your confidence is going to be up and you'll believe in yourself that you can do the rest. You'll feel better and you'll look better. Then we can address the second twenty pounds at that point."

Sometimes a potential member's time-frame goals are too unrealistic. If that happens, utilize your training and experience to help them understand and accept a healthy time-frame:

"That's a very tough task that you're about to undertake. Losing that much weight too quickly is not healthy weight-loss and could be dangerous. Let's break it down a little bit. Let's break that down to two or three pounds per week and see how long it's going to take you to lose that twenty pounds and we'll go from there."

Remember, you are the authority in this situation. Make sure a person is not trying to hurt themselves with an unrealistic time-frame to building muscle or losing fat.

If You're Young and Fit

Many men and women in fitness sales are young, fit, and energetic about it. Older adults who are out of shape may not be in their comfort zone speaking with you. They may be intimidated and put up their defenses. If this is the case, make sure you are very professional in the interaction. Don't read straight off the profile and act like you're filling out a questionnaire. Get the customer involved with the conversation. *Don't do all the talking!*

Lead the Way

At this point in the conversation, be sure you lead the way toward their fitness goals:

> "Look, what I'd like to do ... you need to trust me on this. I need to know where you want to be, where you are starting, and where you want to be to get you in a program that is going to work for you. If you are ready to change your life, if you are ready to take this next step, I'm the one who is going to get you started."

Potential members need to hear that. They need somebody to take control. That is why some of these boot camp programs work, because people can't do it themselves. They are struggling and need somebody to take hold of them and get them started:

> "What I'd like to do is this: I need some answers, your starting point, your finishing point, and I am going to find the shortest distance to that finishing point for you so you can be comfortable. I have been doing this a long time, and I've sat with a lot of people in your situation. I've got some great success stories that I can go over with you right now if you would be interested, if it would make you feel more comfortable. What I would like to do is make you one of my success stories."

Effective Tours

When the time comes for a tour of the facility, make sure you have the basics in your mind. Do they want childcare? Are they interested in group fitness classes? Be sure to emphasize the areas they are most interested in, but tell the potential member that you are going to show them the whole facility. Use the tour to (1) overcome concerns, and (2) make small talk to build rapport. Be sure to play on the positives:

> *It's close to work:* "That's great, because what most people find is that working out during their lunch break, right before work or right after work, they have a tendency to get more workouts in which is a difference between a successful program and an unsuccessful program. So what you'll probably do is come right over here right after work, right?"
>
> *It's close to home:* "The great thing about living right here is that a lot of people find they might miss a workout during the week, they have great intentions, but now you're right next door and you can come in on Saturday or Sunday and take a class or catch up on your workout."

The Power of the Tour

When it is time to close the deal it will be much easier if you have overcome as many objections as possible while conducting the tour and if you have always assumed the sale. Here is a sample of what a tour might sound like. Note the phrases in italics and then take some time to write down afterward how those phrases help point toward the close of the sale:

"Is this membership just for you or for you and someone else? *Great, now that I have found out this is just for you and what you are looking to accomplish* let me show you the facility. Before we start I should make sure you don't have to ask anyone's permission to start a membership. I don't want to waste your time if you aren't the decision maker. You wouldn't believe how many people come in here to shop for a membership but have to ask their mom or spouse if it is okay to start getting fit. I'll give you the tour, I'll *answer all your questions*, and then when we come back *I'll show you how we can get you started* on a membership. This club may look like it is expensive to join, but rest assured we have very affordable packages for every budget. A great thing about our club is that you will have no problem getting started today and achieving your goals. I get excited every time someone comes in to start an exercise program because there is nothing better than seeing someone's body and health be reformed. You are going to be a completely different person in a month. Now that is exciting.

"First I am going to show you the equipment. It's the *best equipment that money can buy*, and we've got a *large line* of equipment. The thing I like best about our equipment is that it is incredibly efficient. The efficiency is going to allow you to get in and out quickly. Most people increase their energy significantly and sleep as much as an hour and a half less every night and are much more productive during the day. Your total exercise program will take less than an hour. You are going to gain as much as a half an hour a day. A lot of people say they don't have time to exercise which as you know now just isn't true. The first line you will be using here is called Paramount; it's got lumbar supports for your back, and it's very easy to adjust. When you are working with a trainer, what he or she will do is come through and show you how to use it properly, how to have proper posture, how to breathe, and how to make sure you're working your muscles and *not straining* your joints. As you can see on the front it actually tells how to adjust the seat according to your height. Come on through this way, and as you can see there is a large line of this kind of equipment. We have *enough equipment to suit all your needs.* There is plenty of it so you *do not have to worry* about waiting for anything. Some of the other clubs in our area have waits as long as 30 minutes for a machine. I'm sure your time is worth much more than that which makes our rates even more cost effective.

"Now, we're open from 4:30 in the morning until 11:00 at night, so you're *never going to have to worry about waiting* for anything, or lines, or having to wait on a piece of equipment. You said you are going to be training at 6:00 in the morning so we know the hours are great for you.

"We also have a line of equipment called Hammer Strength. Hammer Strength is used in all *professional athletic facilities* for their athletes. It is built by computers and all the resistance is independent so if you have a predominantly stronger side of your body it is not going to be doing all the work. That way, everything is balanced. It is a very popular line of equipment and we have 11 pieces in the facility. Hammer Strength even makes *customized equipment* for certain athletic movements. They even make a stand-up bench press for linebackers so when they are pushing, they are pushing forward and it is lifting a weight stack behind them. That way, when they are out on the field pushing 300 and 400 lb. guys around it increases their strength for those movements. It is a very, very popular line of equipment.

"And as you can see, there is *a lot of equipment* available for your use. We have machines that strengthen the abdominal wall and we have machines that strengthen your lower back. You are going to hear a lot from the trainers about core stability and core strength, and it is *a very important part of being in total shape.* So they are manufacturing a lot of equipment to work on strengthening your core. And we've brought some cardiovascular equipment downstairs around the widescreen TV. The whole concept of having cardiovascular around televisions or something to read is that it *takes your focus off of what you are doing,* so you last a heck of a lot longer. Personally, I can't do cardio unless I'm watching television or have something to read—it drives me crazy. And if you don't like what is on this channel, we have *another eight television screens* upstairs with a variety of different channels to watch. *You're not going to get bored* watching the same thing; you have a variety to choose from.

"We also have a Tread wall, which is a natural cardiovascular apparatus that rotates as you're climbing up. You can adjust the pitch and you can adjust the speed, and it's a great work out. When they first brought it in I thought it was going to be great for the kids until I tried it. It's an *awesome workout.* I lasted about fifteen minutes. My forearms were rocks, so it is an awesome workout.

"Over here we have the group fitness room. We have a *variety of classes* you will be choosing from. It's a low-impact floor. We have classes at noon on Monday, Wednesday, and Friday. We have Yoga, we have Pilates, and we have a class called Chisel. Chisel is a very popular class, especially for beginners like yourself. It is very easy to learn. In that class you are basically weight training for an hour. There is no jumping or dancing and it *doesn't take a lot of coordination* so it is easy for beginners to get into. And for people who are looking to metabolize or burn fat, firm and tone muscle, or build muscular endurance, it is a very popular class. We have those classes at 5:30 in the evening Monday through Friday.

"As a permanent member you have *access to all our locations*, and our location just 5 miles away has a high-impact aerobic floor. They offer 30-35 exercise classes a week. This club is near your work and that one is near your home. You can't beat that convenience. The classes vary from Pilates, to yoga, to a dance oriented class called "Zoomba." They have the chiseled class and they have a walking class that meets three times a week. The club 12 miles south of here also offers 30-plus classes a week. So you have *access to all locations, all services and amenities.* We also have Spinning classes at most of our facilities, which is an exercise class done on a stationary bike. It is a very intense class, so I don't recommend that for beginners. I wouldn't suggest you jump right into it, but after a few months it might be great. It is a very popular class.

"As you can see there is a *large variety of cardiovascular equipment* to choose from. I find it amusing that most people think we got this stuff for three easy payments of $29.95 like these are a bunch of home-gym equipment. Our dues rates are much lower than most people's cable bill even though most of these machines cost more than $5,000 a piece. You're *never going to get bored* doing the same old thing every time. Everything is built to be really *easy on your joints.* The value received from your membership is immeasurable. The treadmills are flex-deck treadmills, so even if you are getting up to a pretty good pace it bounces so that it is easy on your joints. It is a lot *safer to run indoors* than it is outdoors because the surface area that you are running on never changes.

"All of the treadmills and most of the cardiovascular equipment have *heart rate monitors built-in.* As I covered before, if you are not hitting your target heart rate when you are doing your cardiovascular workouts, then your body is not metabolizing fat efficiently. That means you are kind of wasting your time. The *last thing we want to have you do is waste time* while you're doing your cardiovascular workouts. These silver handles in the front monitor your heart rate. There is a little box up on front that says "heart rate." Let's say you are working out at 129 beats per minute. Now if your target rate is between 121 and 135, then you are going at the correct speed in order for your body to metabolize fat.

"The elliptical trainers are very popular because the rotary movement takes *all the stress off your joints,* plus you can get an upper body workout as well. And one of my personal favorites is a recumbent exercise bike. I like it simply because it *takes absolutely no coordination* to use. You just sit down with your feet out in front of you, with a place for a reading rack, your water bottle, and a place for your walkman or iPod. And they have heart-rate monitors built in as well. So, they're very easy-to-use, and you can still hit your target heart rate. They are really good for anyone who has *lower back issues* which is pretty common. For people that really need a cardiovascular workout but have a hard time sitting or standing upright, this is the best thing for them, and we have *plenty to choose from.* You *never have to worry* about waiting for anything, which is nice. With our three locations within 25 miles, you *never have to worry* about crowds or overcrowding or having to wait for anything. It disperses the amount of people that we have to work with very nicely.

"As you can see, this is the free weight section. We've got a wide variety of free weights. Our dumbbells range from 3 lbs. to 75 lbs. We pretty much have everything you need. Your training program will probably be 60% free weight training, 40% selectorized training when you are working with a trainer. Again, they will show you proper movements, proper posture, and how to *get the most out of the time* that you are here. Again, the last thing we want you to do is waste time. We want you to *get results as quickly as possible.*

"I'll go on and show you our tanning facilities and I'll show you some of the spa facilities and the amenities there. We have tanning for our members. We have two stand-up beds and two lay-down beds which are a very popular part of the program. They're really nice. They have *their own stereo system* built into the side, and you can plug in your own CD or you can listen to the radio. You can stand up if you want to, and there are fans on the inside on the top and the bottom *so it keeps you really cool.* All you do is take off your clothes, put on your tanning lotion, and stand up. It even tans you underneath your arms. The nice thing is, you're not lying in a pool of your own sweat when you are done, and you are *in and out of here in ten minutes.* They are really popular, and our members use them all the time.

"This is our locker room facilities: *very nice, clean* locker rooms. The lockers are set up on a per-visit basis. You bring a lock with you (most people attach a lock to their gym bag or their backpack), lock your things up while you're here, and take it with you when you leave. We have locker room checks six or seven times per day to keep the facilities really clean. We wipe down the sinks and the mirrors, pick up the things on the floor, and make sure the members have their paper products and things like that.

"Back here we have showers, and we have a steam room right across from the showers. Steam is a very good surface cleaner, it is *very good for your skin* and very good for your complexion. It is also good for your lungs—some people believe that if you're inhaling 120-degree steam then a lot of the toxins in your lungs go out when you exhale. I like it because it is *very, very relaxing* and *very good for stress.*

"Back here we have a Jacuzzi hot tub, which is also very relaxing. It is great for stress, or if you have a sprain or a pulled muscle, or if you just want to *relax after a long day.* Think of it this way: if you work out for forty-five minutes, come into the steam room for ten minutes and the hot tub for ten minutes, you are literally going to float home. You will feel great. And for *security and safety* purposes, we have a window where we can always look in and make sure everything is safe and everybody is okay.

"That's pretty much it. Now that you've seen the facility, do you have any other questions about the services, amenities, the equipment, the hours, anything at all?"

During the tour it is important to be enthusiastic and continue getting yeses. Paint a picture of a new body and life for the person you are touring. Paint a picture of how differently people will treat the new member and some of the things co-workers and peers will say.

Words Can Make a Difference

Take a moment now to think about how this tour was performed. Was it effective? Why or why not? How did some of the phrases used (shown above in italics) point toward a close of a sale?

Write some of your thoughts below.

_____

_____

_____

_____

_____

_____

_____

_____

_____

_____

_____

Now read some of the words and phrases used in this tour and how they build on each other and how they emphasize the benefits of a yes:

now that I have found out what you are looking to accomplish
answer all your questions
I'll show you how we can get you started
best equipment that money can buy
large line
not straining
tells how
enough equipment to suit all your needs
do not have to worry
never going to have to worry about waiting
professional athletic facilities
customized equipment
a lot of equipment
a very important part of being in total shape
takes your focus off of what you are doing
another eight television screens
you're not going to get bored

awesome workout.
a variety of classes
doesn't take a lot of coordination
access to all our locations
access to all locations, all services and amenities
large variety of cardiovascular equipment
never going to get bored
easy on your joints
safer to run indoors
heart rate monitors built-in.
last thing we want to have you do is waste time
all the stress off your joints,
takes absolutely no coordination
lower back issues
plenty to choose from
never have to worry
get the most out of the time
get results as quick as possible
your own stereo system
it keeps you real cool.
in and out of here in ten minutes.
very nice, clean
very good for your skin
very, very relaxing
very good for stress.
relax after a long day
security and safety

A Totally Different Story

It is possible to show someone around a facility without integrating the kinds of words and phrases that the tour above had. Read the following example of a shorter tour and think about what you could have said that would have made a difference in closing a sale afterward:

> "Let me show you around. Let's start off with machine weights and Paramount equipment. We have everything from a leg curl to a chest press and the works. Right here we have our cardio equipment area. We have stair climbers, and elliptical machines. Next up are the bikes. We have the recumbent bikes as well as the regular bikes, treadmills, and some brand new starter-track treadmills.

> "Let's head to aerobics. This is our yoga class. We have to be quiet because they are meditating.

> "In the locker room we have pretty big lockers.

"This is the free weight room. It is for people that are serious about results. Free weights burn three times as many calories as machine weights do. We have a full line of Hammer String which are very good machines, as well as other machines including cable machines.

"We have a couple of squat racks as well as smith racks. We have inner/outer thigh machines that are very popular.

"This is the Spinning room. It has been proven to burn the most calories. Spinning is a 45-minute class. In the class you end up trying as hard as you can because you have someone less than a foot away from you sweating and trying as hard as they can to push the limits.

"We have four tanning beds. Two are lay-down, two are stand-up. The lay-downs are the low pressure beds and they go for about twenty minutes. The stand ups here are the most popular because you get the most even tan."

From start to finish, this was an entirely different tour. It was a shorter tour, of course, but even on a shorter tour in a smaller facility you must speak to the following issues:

(1) your knowledge and experience, (2) the cleanliness and safety of the facility, (3) the help that a member will receive in learning the equipment, (4) the personal training available to members, (5) the benefits of different types of exercise, (6) the benefits of membership such as stress reduction, weight loss, and self-image, (7) the quality of the equipment on the floor, (8) tips to avoiding boredom, and (9) how to work out as efficiently as possible.

Utilizing a fitness profile and an effective tour are critical pieces of the sales process. If you short circuit either of them or perform them in a substandard way, you will be less likely to close the sale. Think about the way you interview potential members and how you tour your facility. Write down your strengths and weaknesses in each area and how you would like to work on those areas:

Fitness Profile Interview

My key strength:

How I will maximize my strength this month:

My key weakness:

How I will improve my weakness this month:

Touring the Facility

My key strength:

How I will maximize my strength this month:

My key weakness:

How I will improve my weakness this month:

Notes:

_____

_____

_____

_____

_____

_____

_____

_____

_____

_____

_____

_____

_____

_____

_____

_____

Chapter 7:
Getting to the Close & Overcoming Objections

How Does That Sound?

No matter what close you are using, regardless of pricing or price structure, and no matter what special is currently running, eventually you are going to say these words, or something like them: *How does that sound?* It's pretty basic.

Here are some common objections you will bump into when it comes time to close. Read over them, and try to imagine how you'd respond to each objection. Then, read over some example responses throughout the chapter.

1. *"You know, I really want to talk to my wife first."*

2. *"I don't have the money for this right now."*

3. *"I don't have the time."*

4. *"I'm worried about a contract."*

Be a closer!

Whatever phrase you use, end your presentation. And then you're done ... until they say something! Be very quiet at that point. The potential member is thinking. *Hey, he just asked me for a commitment to join right now.* Of course, they feel a little bit of pressure in the process. Don't be a hard closer. Don't be a mean closer. But be a closer!

If you think they are ready, put the price in front of them and ask, "How does that sound?" Then, wait for him or her to say something. "Ummm," "I don't know," "I don't think so," or "Yes." If he or she says "Yes," then obviously drop right into the paperwork. If they say nothing for a minute or two, that is unbearable pressure on them. The longer they are quiet, the more pressure it is! Don't be tempted to break the silence. If you add, "And remember, the kids club is included" it gives them a chance to breathe a little bit.

The longer the wait, the more serious they are about doing it. If they don't say yes right away and they are still thinking while they are looking at it, and then let them wait. They are just making the decision in their mind. If they don't want to join, they will tell you, and then you can take the next step.

The closes that you should be using are very basic and can all segue into other things you say and do. There is no trick to it. They are very easy; common-sense things you say to people that will make a lot of sense both to you and to them.

An Example

One example I use in training is of a woman who is overweight and who has never been in a gym. She is divorced from her husband of twenty five years, a little bitter about it, and she wants to change her life. She needs your help. If at that point you have done everything right and she is still saying, "I don't think so" then there is a reason for it. Sometimes you have to come right at them and ask them why. If you ask them a question such as, "Marcia, does that make sense? You're here, you like the facility, your goals are realistic. Doesn't it make sense that we get you started today? Why wait for a month, a year ... if you get started today you are going to feel different in a month. If you wait a month, you are not going to feel any different. We can get you started right now. Doesn't that make sense?" Now you are back to getting her to say "Yes."

If you are down to everything and it seems like it is going well, you can give a potential member a little bit of a scapegoat by saying, "Look, Marcia, it is one of two things ... it's either the money, and we haven't really gone over all of your options yet because I haven't gotten you to say yes yet ... or it's your commitment. Are you serious about changing your life? Are you serious about doing this? Or are you concerned that you can't get started? Because if it is your commitment, let me get you started. Let me help you with that. I'll call you three times a week to tell you to get down here if you want me to."

Of course, if you offer to call someone three times a week, then call them three times a week! Don't offer if you are not serious because you need to keep your word. If the man or woman says, "If you do that I'll join" then make sure you follow up. Call three times a week and say, "When was the last time you were at the club?"

Reassurance

As a potential member sits and feels the pressure of the sale, make sure you believe what you are saying. And make sure you reassure her or him.

Objection 1:

"You know, I really want to talk to my wife first."

"Great, I'm glad that you want to talk to her. It shows that you are serious about it, but, let me mention something to you ... the average woman, in any given month, between what they spend on their hair, their fingernails, and their make-up ... it is probably $150 bucks a month. A month."

"Yeah, I know."

"Okay, does she ask you, 'Honey can I get my nails done, can I get my hair cut, can I buy some make-up?'"

"Never"

"No. And why does she spend money on that stuff?"

"Cause it makes her feel good."

"Makes her feel good and look better ... let's get you started."

"Alright."

"I understand how you feel because a lot of people who have sat in that seat that I have helped have felt the same way. What we found was that this is the toughest part, Marcia. You have to take that next step, you have to join and get yourself down here to work out. If you do that, you're going to change. You are going to feel better, you're going to look better, and we just have to take that next step." Give them some reassurance. At that point you may want to call in a manager for a take-over (sometimes called a turn-over). He or she will not have had the opportunity to built rapport so the manager will come across as the harder closer.

You may, however, be able to utilize the pressure to your advantage. Here are some basic things you can say that will reel the potential member back in:

"Look, I understand. I can tell by your body language and I can see that you are getting a little uncomfortable with this. That's my job and I have done this a lot. Marcia, what I have found is that if I push you a little bit harder and you join and you lose those twenty pounds and you change your life, I am going to be your best friend. But if I don't push you a little harder and you walk out of here and six months from now you are still not working out and you're feeling worse and you are walking back through the door wishing you had joined now, that doesn't do any one of us any good. So I'm going to leave it up to you: do I keep pushing, do I keep trying to get you to join right now and make this next step, or do you want me to back off? Because if you want me to back off then say so."

Objection 2:

"I don't have the money for this right now."

"We are looking at $99, the processing, you never have to pay this again, and this is just to get you started. With first and last months dues, the total comes to $256. How does that work into your scheme of things?"

"$256 today?"

"Yeah."

"And $39 a month?"

"Mmmhmm. About as much as you spend on a night out at a ... go to a pizza parlor."

"That's a lot of money though. The $256 down is a lot of money, I just don't have that kind of money right now."

"But you want to get started right?"

"Yeah."

"Okay, so if there is a way that I could work out the $256 so that you could make it in a couple of installments, would that work out for you?

"How much are we lookin' at?"

"How close can you come to the $256 today?"

"I only have like $30 on me right now."

"And you could part with that?"

"Yeah."

"If I could get the authorization to take the $30, and we could break up the balance of the installments on the 31st of this month and the 15th of next month ... would that work out for you?"

Typically in this situation, half of the potential members say, "I don't want to join. I need time to think about it." Back off. Set them up with a pass, introduce them to your front desk, and make them feel comfortable. You may even want to say, "Marcia, the worst part of this whole thing is the sales stuff. This is the hardest part, but that is what we do. You'll be happy to join, you'll love the club, and our front desk is really nice. But for now let's get you set up with a pass and let's get you started. I can set up an appointment for the end of the month and we'll go over all of this sales stuff. By then you will know the price, and you'll know that you want to do it. Because if you use this club you are going to feel better. In two weeks this will be an easy decision because you won't believe how good you will feel after two weeks. Just imagine two months and two years! You'll wish you would have started today. But, let's go ahead and get you set up for the end of the month. I'll get you started on the pass. How does that sound?'

If the customer forces you to back off, then back off. Make sure everybody is nice to him or her on the way out the door. Just because you think you lost the sale doesn't mean that you should blow it here. Be nice to this person and they may still join at the end of the month! Remember, if you're a good sales person you will remember her name, and talk to her when she comes in to use the facilities. If you don't see her, follow up a week later and say, "Marcia, did you use the club this week?" Maybe she came in early and no one saw her. If she didn't use the club, encourage her. "Marcia, I know that you know you have to do this."

Remember, through the whole process—through the profile, the tour, the sales presentation—one of the things you are going to find is that sometimes

Objection 3:

"I don't have the time."

"It's probably the single biggest, now don't be offended, probably the single biggest excuse that we hear. But look at it this way, there are 168 hours in a week, 168 hours in a week ... all I really want from you is 4 ... 4 hours out of 168 hours in a week Let me ask you this: how many hours do you spend in front of a TV screen, whether it's playing video games or watching TV?"

"You know, really not that much."

"Really."

"You know, I don't watch TV that much, I spend most of my time with my kid."

"Do you think your kid wants you to be healthy? You want to be around for your kids, your grandkids, things like that?"

"Oh yeah, most definitely."

"It has to be the top priority in your life, Paul. It has to be 4 hours, whether its getting up an hour earlier 3 or 4 times a week, or utilizing your time more constructively on your lunch hours, or just telling your wife 'Hey honey, I'm getting home an hour later 3 or 4 times a week, but I'm going to look my best and feel my best. It has to be your top priority. Let's get you started."

"Okay."

through your body language and/or the words you say you are going to unintentionally tie them down.

Make sure they are still involved in the conversation. Don't only ask closed-ended questions with only "yes" or "no" answers. Don't direct them too much that you can't pull the information from them. An example of a tie-down is if they don't know you have kids and you walk through the kid's club and it is all neat and orderly and at the end of that you just say, "Isn't this a great kid's club?" You want them to say, "Yes it is," so your body language is going to be positive, smile, and with that body language they will feel it and they will get on board with you. So as the process goes along you are still going to ask questions with a "yes" answer but also be sure to ask some open-ended questions to get to know them a little bit more and not tie them down.

People Are Not A Number

A couple points to remember is that behind every sale there is a *person* back there. People have goals! Don't address an interaction as, "This will be my fifth person today to get to join!" because although you may have five people that day, this may be the one time this person walks into the gym to think about joining. Make them comfortable.

If you treat them like they are a number then your sales rate is going to gradually decrease over time compared to if you genuinely interact with that

---

Objection 4:

*"**I'm worried about a contract.** You know, in my last health club I had to sign up for a certain amount of time ... is there a contract involved?"*

"Well, I don't know, I prefer to call it an agreement. I'm agreeing to provide you a service, and get you in the best shape of you life ... you're end is to pay for it. It is a 12 month membership."

"Oh, Okay."

"After the 12 months Paul, you can keep going for as long as you want, and most people do. But initially, all I want you to do is turn your body over to us for 12 months, not your whole life."

"You know, that's a long time to sign up for, I mean, you know ... "

"It's a long time to stay in shape. Let me put it this way Paul, I'm going to be working out at the Fitness Center for the rest of my life. They will probably find me floating in the hot tub in my 90s, hopefully in my hundreds, because it's just a way of life. Stopping exercising in the Fitness Center would be like stopping brushing my teeth, and you have to look at it that way. You're basically saying 'I'm not sure I want to stay in shape for the rest of my life.' It sounds pretty stupid doesn't it?"

"Yeah, it does."

"Let's get you started."

"Okay."

---

person. Deep down, every person wants to be respected! And they are not in your club to buy one-hundred pieces of cardio equipment. They are only interested in the piece that will help them lose twenty pounds. Find out what their goals are, and deal with that person the right way. Help them get what they want! It might be your one opportunity to help this person change their life. Spend the time with them and build rapport. Treat them like a human being! And when you give them a membership, make sure they know they will have the support to change their life.

Notes:

_____

_____

_____

_____

_____

_____

_____

_____

_____

_____

_____

_____

_____

_____

_____

_____

_____

_____

Chapter 8:
Points to Consider in Successful Sales

In addition to overcoming objections, there are several other elements which, in combination, help create an environment where successful sales occur. Remember, your fitness center is built on sales. And sales are built on a solid foundation incorporating the following elements and understanding these issues:

The Mission Statement

One of the first things you should have your sales reps do is memorize your mission statement. And if your company does not have one, write one! Mission statements help clarify for employees what you are—and what you are not. Why you exist. And if that is learned and embodied by your staff, then that will "leak" through to your members.

Think back to a time when you worked somewhere with a fair degree of unity. A time when most of the employees at a particular business had teamwork and synergy together. Now, what happened when an existing employee or a new hire came on who did not have the same set of values or mission about why the company existed? And how did that trickle down to the customers you served? Typically, if employees don't understand the single unifying vision as to why your company exists, your customers or members will get a mixed message and your ability to keep and grow your customer base will be hindered.

Having your sales staff *memorize* your mission statement is critical. Why? Because not only will it force the team to learn your mission as an organization, but it will also develop a sense of belief in the mission which will affect the team's ability to be consistent with the way they treat people in and around the clubs.

If you have a mission statement, try this: casually ask people at various levels of the organization about your mission. What is the statement? What is the mission of your organization? Write down their answers and ask yourself what consistencies appear and what discrepancies appear. The answers you receive will tell you a lot about how well your business is executing its purpose and mission.

Are You Talking to a Qualified Buyer?

Presuming you understand the mission of your organization, you will need to have good communication skills as you speak with your contacts. And through small talk you will begin to understand whether you are talking to a qualified buyer.

If you ask about their work, stretch that out a little bit. If they say, "I've been with my company for ten years and love my job," then that's a qualified buyer. People do not work in a job for ten years if it pays poorly and they're not very stable. If they say, "I just got hired at my job," you may want to ask a couple more questions to learn if that person is going to be there for very long. Look for signs of stability as you speak to them about what they are looking for in a membership.

Don't Turn Cold

If you find out that someone does not live or work near your facility, and he or she walked in because they were killing time before a meeting nearby, don't turn cold. If you act right away as though you don't want to deal with them because you found out they were not a buyer, that is a mistake. Instead, skip over the profile and give them a tour of the facility. *Be as nice as you can be to that person.* Why? Because that person may walk into their meeting and talk about the woman or man at the health club. "He treated me great even though I don't live here. He showed me the facility, it's a great club, and the guy was really nice." You have the opportunity to affect potential members even if you aren't speaking to a qualified buyer!

Married Couples

Let's say that you're speaking to a married woman about a membership. Ask her, "Is the membership going to be just for you, or for you and your husband?" If she says, "It's just for me" then you can move on. If the membership is for both, respond this way:

> "Great, does he know you are here taking a look at the facility, and does he trust you to get the membership started for both of you?"

If she says, "No, he would have to make his own decision," then that's a no.

> "Great, I'm going to show you the facility, go over some options, and we can get you started. I can give him a pass for the month and we can just add him on your membership later."

If the answer is still no, you are getting to the point now where you are going to respond this way:

> "No problem. What I would like to do now is let you take a look at the facility and I could set up a time for your husband to come back and we'll do this same process with him, I'll give him a tour. How does that sound?"

You are looking for a yes. At that time if she says, "No, I'm just going to take prices and go home" then ask her what she thinks of the facilities so far. If she likes them, ask her if she thinks she wants to be a member. If she does, say this:

> "Then why don't you let me do my job, and bring your husband in here. He will love the facility, and I'll go over his options. I am sure I'll get you two started.

I know so many people who regretted taking the price sheet home to their spouses. They got shot out of the water when they *really wanted a membership for themselves.* The spouse found too many excuses not to workout and they were never members.

You have to do it today?

Avoid the pressure tactic of "today" thinking. People are getting too marketing-savvy for that kind of tactic. Instead, explain the benefits. Address the promotions that you currently have, the advantages of joining today, perhaps you can give them a better value if they joined soon.

When Your Customer is Overwhelmed

Your sales reps are typically strong and fit, or at least pursuing their own personal fitness goals to build muscle and/or lose weight. They are gym people. They walk around a facility and typically know what the equipment is for and how it is used.

As you tour the facility and address objections it's easy to talk about convenience, the spouse issue, the money issues. But a larger facility can be very intimidating to people. They may not bring up that concern, but it's your responsibility to bring it up. Many people won't want to or don't know how to articulate this concern. Don't wait for them to say something such as, "I wouldn't know where to start."

Take Dave, for example. Dave was a bicyclist. He biked for exercise while in college, took a few years off and then picked it back up awhile later. He trained to be able to finish a community bike race once, and if he ever had time to "exercise," he rode his bike. It's the only thing he really enjoyed or felt like doing. When he thought about joining a gym, he was most interested in the cardio equipment, specifically the bikes. He wanted to be able to bike indoors during the winter, or early in the morning when it was dark. He was a nice guy, comfortable in his own skin, and confident. But the majority of the gym floor *freaked him out.* You wouldn't know from looking at Dave that it would be an objection, but it was. He wanted more muscle mass and more definition. He wanted his biceps to show through his T-shirt sleeves. He wanted to look great in board shorts at the ocean. But he was overwhelmed by the equipment at the gym and didn't know where to start. He didn't feel terribly out of shape and he was only a few pounds heavier than he wanted to be. But the thought of fumbling around with the equipment on the floor while guys who were *ripped* walked around confidently was too much for him. He didn't want to feel stupid.

In your conversation make sure you reassure the man or women you are speaking with:

"Hey, I know that this floor can look very intimidating and I know that this is a lot of equipment. We are going to make sure you get settled into a program and we are going to show you how to use the equipment. I'm not going to give you a piece of paper and kick you out on the floor. Hey look, everybody started like you are right now. Everybody came in and was brand new in this gym, they did not know where to start and they had to take that first step. If you really want to change your life, if you really want to get going you've got to take the next step. Maybe the first time or two you are not quite in your comfort zone, but a couple months from now you'll have it all down and you'll know all this equipment. You will have lost some weight and you'll look better. You'll feel better too."

The opposite is also true. You might be speaking to an 18-year-old muscle guy who is just switching gyms and does not care much about the group classes or the kids area. On the tour he might just say, "I don't even need to look in there because I don't have kids." Show him the entire facility anyway!

You can say to him, "Hey look, you probably have friends that have kids and you never know. So I want to show you. I'm very proud of this kid's club area, and that way if you have any friends that want to know if we have kids club you can let them know what you thought about it. So do me a favor and come and look at this with me." You can do the same thing with the aerobics area. There are two benefits to this: one, you are able to make connections with people he might know who would use those areas, and two, if he complains about the price of his membership to use only the free weights you can explain the overhead for the entire facility, not just the part of the facility he has seen and wants to use. That way he is not trying to compare apples to oranges if he is comparing your club to a club down the street that only features free weights and little else.

Going Over Options

If the tour has gone well and you've collected a lot of yeses, the end of the tour is the time for them to make their commitment.

> "So, what did you think of this facility?"
>
> "Do you see yourself getting a workout here?"
>
> "Great, then what I'd like to do is sit down and go over your options. We've got a great promotion going on right now, and we can get you started."

If they are resistant, follow up on it a little bit without being rude. It's likely that at the beginning of the tour you had a hard time figuring out where the person was coming from, and by the end of the tour hopefully you have had the opportunity to build a rapport. If you've done your job building rapport, the potential member would say anything to you.

Leadership Development

As a sales representative of the company, you always want to be working on self-leadership. Self-leadership is your ability to lead yourself, develop and grow in your task or craft.

One book many sales reps have found helpful is How to Win Friends and Influence People by Dale Carnegie (Pocket Books/Simon & Schuster). This basic book is full of ideas on how to work on your interactions with people. It's also helpful if you struggle with a personal weakness of losing your temper easily or getting defensive. It will help you in your interactions with people and keep the focus on the other person instead of yourself.

Do Favors for Members

One of the best ways to connect with people is through doing favors for them. This is something that you can start on your first day at the club.

Walk-throughs are obviously critical to health club management. It helps you make sure the club is clean and so members know you are there. But one of the best results of consistent walk-through is connecting with and building relationships with members who are using the club regularly.

Be sure to get to know the members who use the club daily. Take time to get to know the members. If they bring their children in with them each time, learn the names of their kids! Connecting and learning the names of members makes them feel good, and helps them have a good experience. It also makes your job easier—the more people you know, the more comfortable you are, and the better your work environment.

In addition to learning who your members are, it is also important to do favors for members. What is a favor? If a member comes up to you and asks you if you can spot for them on the bench, and you say yes, that is *not* a favor. They are hoping for or expecting a "yes" answer. If you walk by and offer to spot for them, however, that is a favor. They are not asking for or expecting your help. A favor is *beyond what is expected* by a member.

If your focus is sales, it is easy to focus on potential members and forget your responsibility toward the members your club already has. But getting to know your existing members and doing favors for them will increase your satisfaction in your workplace and grow your customer base over time.

Go Over and Above

One of the differences between someone who is working a job and someone who is going beyond that is how they approach tasks which are not their responsibility—yet. If you want more than just a job—if you want a career, dig into the process from the start.

Ask yourself about different processes and tasks that need to be done regularly: what are the logs, what is the evening paperwork, what are the responsibilities you may have several months from now? Do what you can do learn those quickly. You never know when there is going to be an emergency or a meeting and a manager will turn to you and say, "I wish you knew how to fill out this paperwork" and you can say confidently, "I do."

You probably will not be pressured to learn a lot of the process paperwork in your first few weeks or months. But you would do well to learn what you can when you can. You might not be expected to pick up the ball and run with it right away, but your supervisor will definitely be aware and receptive to you wanting to learn as much as you can as quickly as you can.

Conclusion

I realize that this is a lot to chew on, dealing with various issues such as married couples, insecurities, developing your own skills and going all out for your members. As you learn and grow in sales, there are several things to remember! As a whole, a greater understanding of these issues will not only help improve your personal bottom line (fatter paycheck), but they will grow the business and bring in a steady flow of new members.

Look back through these various issues and details in sales. What areas require more work from you or from the people you lead? Which areas do you have dialed in fairly well? Begin now to increase your understanding and training in these areas and pursue them with strength and commitment:

Two areas from this chapter which are strengths of mine:

My plan to maximize my strengths this month:

Two areas from this chapter which are weaknesses of mine:

My plan to improve upon my weaknesses this month:

Notes:

SECTION THREE:

KEEPING & GROWING YOUR CUSTOMER BASE

Chapter 9:
The Gift Bag

A gift bag is an incredible way to build your business and create synergy among local businesses in your community. It is not easy at first but the simplicity of the principle, rightly applied, will create so much business for you that you won't look back.

If you spoke to some of the most successful fitness club chains across the country, they would probably say that the gift bag concept is too complicated or sounds like too much work. Well, when you start out it does take some work. And it can be complicated. But once you get it down *it is simple.*

Making Each Other Successful

The gift bag concept educates companies how you can co-op and make each other successful.

The concept of mutual success drives energy up in both businesses and creates a sense of teamwork that creates results. But at first you might be intimidated or frustrated. The process of making it easy *takes time.* If you are not in your comfort zone with it, if you feel awkward, don't shy away from it just because of that. Take it on as a challenge and be relentless on getting good in this area!

The chain of clubs I worked with for several years had some similarities with other chains and we learned from *what* they do and *how* they do business. We also chucked things we did not think worked very well. But the whole arena of co-ops with other businesses is definitely something that set us apart.

Businesses that advertise want a return on their investment. If they spend $500 they want $1,000 back. They also want a way to track the return on their investment. This is no secret. We want to create value for a company's advertising dollars. If we have the best value, we will obtain a lot of advertising customers.

We have developed what we call the gift bag. The gift bag is made up of a network of businesses promoting each other. The following is a list of businesses that tend to work well. Some restrictions will apply, such as one gift certificate per month per customer.

Yogurt Shops	50-cent gift certificate
Car Washes	$3 gift certificate
Video Stores	$1 gift certificate
Dry Cleaners	2 articles free certificate
Coffee Shops	50-cent gift certificate
Christian Book Stores	$3 gift certificate

Health Clubs	1 month free certificate
Restaurants	1 appetizer
Bike Shops	Trade 2 one year memberships for a mountain bike
Travel Agents	Trade 2 one year memberships for a trip
Landscapers	1 free lawn cut
Beauty Salons	$3 gift certificate
Pizza Parlors	1 pitcher of soda certificate
Auto Dealers	Take a test drive and get a one month membership to xyz club
Ice Cream Shops	50-cent gift certificate
Massage Therapist	20-minute massage certificate
Ad Agencies	

Now, go over the list again and mark next to each one which specific businesses in your community can and should network together to create momentum and promote each other. As an owner of a chain of health clubs, we increased our dues ten-fold with the use of the gift bag!

Many of the ideas and examples here will not be practical or efficient for many health club businesses, but what I've written here will get staff member's creative juices flowing. These ideas are used in our clubs to get general managers and sales counselors brainstorming on how to network market with other businesses. Most of our staff members find variations of these ideas they are more comfortable with or work better for them.

Example One: Advertising Together

The first example I will describe involves advertising in a community newspaper together. First, create a network of businesses. Then, set up advertising in a local or community newspaper. Businesses will contribute to the advertising budget in order to be in the network. All businesses in the network might contribute $300 to a newspaper add and would be listed on a full page ad. The ad would state, "Visit these businesses and receive a free gift." All the businesses in the network are listed on the page together. When a customer visits one of the businesses in the network they get to reach into a large gift bag and pull out a gift certificate to one of the other businesses in the network.

Each business would contribute gift certificates to place in the other businesses' gift bags. The gift certificates are a way for each business to say "thank-you" to their customer. In our clubs, sales counselors are required to do so many favors every two hours. A counselor could go up to a member and say, "I just want to thank you for being a member here. Have you tried the new restaurant downtown? Well, here is an appetizer on us. Just take it down their and tell them I sent you. Here's my card."

When the customer takes the free appetizer gift into the restaurant, the restaurant manager greets the customer and thanks the customer for coming in. He or she might say, "Thanks for coming in today. Please reach into our gift bag and take a gift." "Wow, you've got a $5 gift certificate to the car wash right down the road." When the customer shows up at the car wash the car wash applies the $5 gift certificate to the car wash.

In our clubs we give businesses what we call tricerts. This is a gift certificate for a one-month membership or $199, which is our enrollment. The gift certificate may be applied to our enrollment. The customer puts their name and number on the tricert and we pick them up once a week from all the businesses we have given them to. We call the customers and ask when they would like to activate their membership.

Advertising within the Network

If you want to build a large-ticket item into your gift bag, you can do this by paying for the advertising in the newspaper for the business you want to acquire the item from or you can trade directly. Your club can pay for as much of the ad as a bike costs or give a bike shop the equivalent value in memberships. If the bike shop's portion of the ad is $300 and the bike is $500, the health club could pay the $300 and give the bike shop $200 in memberships. The bike would now go into the club's gift bag. The bike could be raffled off in a drawing where everyone who makes a referral to the club gets a ticket dropped into a raffle box. Each member that brings some in to join would get 5 raffle tickets. This would work the same way for a travel agent. The travel agent throws in a trip and gets two one-year memberships to use in their business.

Other businesses working in the network can be taught to use the same strategies.

Car dealers can be given one-month memberships for anyone that test drives a car. The car dealer can give the health club a $500 gift certificate toward the purchase of a new vehicle also or what ever they choose.

These are some ideas to get people thinking. Once health clubs start brain storming ideas in this area all kinds of good things happen. I recommend discussing any ideas involving trades with a qualified tax professional.

Foot Traffic Within the Network

The more a business contributes to the network, the more a business benefits. If they contribute one hundred 50-cent gift certificates, then over time one hundred people will come in with their families and buy $10 worth of yogurt and apply their 50-cent gift certificate.

Because the yogurt shop is a part of the network, that shop also has a bag full of gifts. So the worker selling the yogurt says, "Thanks for your business! Would you like one of our gifts? We have gift certificates toward car washes, free video rentals, free dry cleaning, free coffee, Christian book store gift certificates, one-month health club memberships and a free appetizer at Joe Bob's restaurant."

All businesses in the gift bag are able to track the success of the network because the gift certificates they give out are returned. All businesses in the network promote each other. The goal should be to have *at least ten* businesses promoting each other by handing out gift certificates.

We have significantly built our business by networking and interacting with businesses. You promote the other businesses and they in turn promote yours. It also works well inside your clubs when you integrate the gift bag concept with doing favors for your members, which I have required of my sales counselors on their *daily checklists*.

Building Your Gift Bag

First you have to *build* a gift bag. Now how do you do that exactly? First, you need to understand that there are some businesses that are better and easier to work with than others. Some good ones are listed previously in this chapter. Think through businesses such as coffee shops, dry cleaners, delis, car washes, etc.

As an owner, manager or employee in the fitness industry, you have something to offer. Not only do you have something that will be a benefit to the businesses that you trade with, it will also benefit you because it promotes you, and what you are giving other places to give out will help promote your club and bring foot traffic into your clubs.

Start with a local coffee shop. Network with the coffee shop and give them fifty tricerts that offer one-month memberships, a personal training session and two tans. This pass is for non-members only and it is for first-time guests. Obviously you want to drive first time guests into your clubs.

What is the coffee shop going to contribute? They contribute a number of gift certificates that can be applied to coffee. Does the owner of the coffee shop want to give away money? Of course not, and health clubs don't either. You are not giving away money with those passes—you are gaining the possibility of a membership. Work with the owner or manager of the café to understand that they will gain foot traffic with the gift certificates. Then, the coffee shop has the opportunity to up-sell. When a person brings a gift certificate in for a coffee they have the opportunity to apply their gift certificate towards a larger coffee or specialty drink:

> *"Would you like a free regular coffee or would you like to use the $1.50 toward a café mocha?"*

The coffee shop gives your club a certain amount of free coffees. Remember, that café is not giving away free money to the gift bag! They are creating foot-traffic and getting an opportunity to *gain a customer through good service and good coffee*. In addition, they also have an opportunity to break even by selling the upgrade.

And guess what happens to customers who go in to buy coffee at the coffee shop?

> *"Thanks for coming in today. We really appreciate your business. And you know what? Here is a free one-month membership over at the fitness center. It's a great club, and with the certificate you get a free one-month membership, two free tans and a free personal training session. It is just our way of saying thank you for coming in and giving us the business."*

Giving Favors to Existing Members

One of the methods of keeping and increasing your customer base is by giving favors to your members. I touched on this subject earlier in the book but I will expand on it here, and how it relates to the gift bag network of businesses.

Coffee, Anyone?

Let's say that a member on the floor is lifting weights and using the machines. Approach the member and greet him:

"Hi, Mr. Smith, how are you today? You know what? I have a gift for you. I just want to say thanks for being a member here and we really appreciate the business. I have a free coffee for you. It's a new café in town over on 15th Street. Go on in and here is a small coffee. Now make sure you give them this gift certificate and my card. I will paperclip them together for you, so Marie knows that I gave it to you and it is not just floating around somewhere it is not supposed to be."

It is important for you to give out your card because now when Mr. Smith goes over and gets a free coffee, Marie will see the consistency of you sending people in. Also, you can track whom you gave coffees to so if the coffee place is not giving out the one-month memberships, then you can either change that or work with a different coffee place that will promote your club. Be the first to give, and then wait to see if the business reciprocates and gives back to you.

Car Wash, Anyone?

Use the same principles with a car wash. Go to the owner or operator of the car wash and give them 50 one-month memberships, the same thing you gave to the coffee shop. In return, get 100 $5 gift certificates for a car wash. At first the owner will not appreciate the offer to give away free money. The car wash has the opportunity to up-sell. When the person shows up at their business, the sales staff has been trained to offer upgrades:

"For an extra $5.00 we can vacuum the inside of the car for you and add a scent of your choice.

This way, the car wash has the opportunity to grow their customer base by giving great service and giving a great car wash. And the car wash also has the opportunity to promote your business when customers come in to buy a car wash:

"Thanks for coming in. We appreciate your business! Here is a one-month membership over at the health club. Are you a member? No? Great, why don't you try it out? It's on us, just our way of saying thanks for coming in."

When a Favor is Not a Favor

I touched on this earlier in the book: some things qualify as a favor and others do not. If you want to keep and grow your customer base, it will do you well to understand the difference.

Go above and beyond the expectations of your members. If you do that, it qualifies as a favor. If you walk up to a member finishing up a workout on a treadmill and offer her water, she would not expect that. That would qualify as a favor. It is above and beyond what a member on a treadmill would expect.

If a member comes up to you and asks you help changing their tire, they expect you to at least help out somehow because otherwise they would not have asked. But what if they say this:

"I have a flat tire. Do you mind if I use your phone? I need to call my wife. I took the jack out of the trunk last weekend when I needed it for something else and I forgot to put it back in when I was done. I need her to bring it down here so I can change the tire."

If you say, "Don't worry about calling. I've got a jack you can use. How about if I go help you out? He is not expecting your help. That qualifies as a favor!

Expanding your Gift Bag

I've written about coffee shops and about car washes. If I were building a bag, I would include quite a few car washes and quite a few coffees in my gift bag.

Start to think about what else you can build into your bag. What else can you find? Go to a local video store that rents DVD's and games. Find a dry cleaners that will network with you.

How would a dry cleaner work in the network? Well, try to get gift certificates for two articles of clothing. Many people dry clean more articles than that unless they are testing out a new store. Many people think, "I have a certificate for two articles; I'm going to take four or five and get two of them free." This way, the dry cleaner has the opportunity to break even or profit from the certificate, in addition to the opportunity to do great business and earn a new customer.

The same principle holds for a restaurant with a certificate for a free appetizer. Approach a popular local restaurant and give them 50 one-month passes and explain the guidelines for the passes, etc. In return, ask them for 150 gift certificates for a free appetizer. How many people do you think are going to go to that restaurant and order the appetizer and a glass of water? Very few! Many people are going to take their spouse or girlfriend or boyfriend out on a date, order an appetizer, a few drinks, and dinner. And the restaurant has the opportunity to profit from the visit as well as earn a return visit from a customer who has a positive experience there.

The gift bag works best when the business gets the name and number of the people who received the one-month pass. This is harder for a restaurant to get, but it works out well for you. You are able to get fifty names and numbers of people who accepted passes and you can call to set appointments. Not having the names and numbers sets you up at a disadvantage, because you cannot start the ball rolling and call to make an appointment. It also creates more distance between you and the other business since you do not know for sure if they handed out all fifty passes. That is why we like to use the *tricerts*. They are filled out at the business. The customer gets the top copy, the sales counselor gets the next copy when he or she picks them up each week and the business keeps the last copy. This is an easy way for a business working with a health club to get a name and phone number.

Tricert

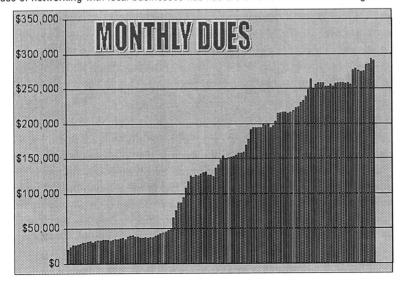

The use of networking with local businesses has had a dramatic affect of increasing our dues base.

The Punch Card

There are a few types of punch cards which I would like to describe here. The first works well with stores like DVD rentals, coffee shops and car washes. Sometimes it is harder to get employees of those stores to give one-month passes because they may not care about promoting your business or about you promoting theirs. Owners and operators tend to care more about that than employees, unfortunately. The other challenge of gift bag trades is that sometimes it is hard to have employees of other stores follow up and get an accurate name and number from people. Sometimes they lie and write down a bogus number; other times the details fall through the cracks and you're simply not able to find out who received the pass.

The punch card works differently. Give a store punch cards. The first 20 people to get their card punched 5 times gets $199 gift certificate toward enrollment. Each customer that comes in to rent a DVD gets the opportunity to receive a punch card. If they return to that business and get their card punched five times, they receive a $199 gift certificate toward enrollment. If the customers know that only the first 20 people to get their cards punched will be rewarded it will cause them to accelerate their movie renting.

It can work differently with different businesses. With the video store, they might have to rent two DVD's or games to receive one punch. So, after five visits and renting two DVD's each time, they receive their gift certificate and save $199. We make it clear that there are only 20 gift certificates available, so everyone with a card knows that the first twenty people who come in with a punched card would receive the certificate. This works well because everyone knows what the reward is, and therefore if they are trying to get their card punched it is because they want a health club membership. The rental store employee will not have to ask to punch the cards. The customers will insist on it!

With a car wash, the concept would work the same way. If people opt-in and take the punch card, they can return to the car wash to get their card punched, and after five washes they receive their gift certificate. The system works well because people self-police the process. They manage the process and make sure they get their card punched when they are supposed to. They do not wait around and expect the clerk at the store to remember to punch their card. They will always know the rules even if an employee doesn't. Like the video store example, the customers know that the first twenty people who turn in the card will receive the gift certificate.

It would work the same way at a café. If someone takes a card, then every time they come in and order a specialty drink, they get their card punched. Whatever rules you set, make sure you stay strict on the rules so you do not devalue the cost of your membership. If you create too many punch cards at various places and have no limits to the number of people who can utilize them, you will create a no-value environment. People will tell each other there really is no enrollment. Everyone gets it waived. All you really have to pay is the processing fee. If someone earns enrollment by getting their card punched, then you've created an excellent network with other businesses and you have created value for both you and them.

A Scavenger Hunt

The second type of punch card works more like a scavenger hunt. If a customer gets their card punched at 4 other business in the network and then bring it in for a 5th punch at the health club, enrollment can be waived. This would be promoted in the other businesses. The businesses working the health club might present it like this:

> "You know what? I have a way that you can save enrollment at the health club. We have a scavenger hunt with other local businesses where you can earn your enrollment fees. This is the way it works: go into these five businesses and purchase something. You can decide what it is. After you visit them, save your receipts and take them to the health club. They will take your punch card and apply it to the enrollment fee. Each time a purchase is made at one of the businesses on the list that business will punch the card. Each time you get your card punched, you get a free workout. After five punches enrollment is waived. How does that sound?"

This is a tool which helps people out who cannot afford your enrollment fees but can afford to pay the monthly membership dues. It is one of many creative ways to help people reduce the initial start-up costs without devaluing the membership. Like the gift bag, your scavenger hunt can include local businesses such as video stores, cafés, and car washes.

Now you have five businesses out there right? What you just gave them is something very valuable. Let's go back to the video store. The video store is one of those businesses that are ideal on the punch card you design. In both cases someone is coming in. In the first scenario they have to rent three movies and receive a punch. Your club is motivating them to rent those three movies, so in return they need to fill up your gift bag.

Tracking Gift Certificates for Membership

Let me emphasis something that is going to make this really efficient. Now, I wrote about it a little bit earlier. You want the names and numbers. It is going to be hard to get other businesses, especially initially, to give you the names and numbers if tricerts are not used. One thing I would recommend is *number the gift certificates*. So lets say you give them 25 or 50 one month memberships, those should have a number on them, a red number or a colored number so that your club can track it and see that it wasn't copied. Now give the business you are working with a gift register. They are going to get a register with 50 names and phone numbers on it from the club when the gifts are distributed at the club. When the business working with the club gives out a health club gift certificate they are going to put that person's name and number on the gift register. So by the time that they give out all 50, there should be 50 names and numbers that match the 50 gift certificates that they gave out. I prefer to spend a little money and use the tricert option.

Remember it's very important for you to show these other businesses that you are doing this, not do as you *say*, but do as you *do*. So likewise you want to have a gift register and every time you give out a gift certificate (maybe it's a coffee or a car wash) you put that person's name and number down and it creates value—that there are only so many of these and we need to know who is getting each one. That will help you out a lot when you go and give that to the businesses you are working with. I recommend that you go in once a week and say, "Can I see the list? I would like to get a copy of it for this week's records."

Outside Appointments at Gift Bag Businesses

Now the other thing that you can do when you develop your gift bag is this: let's say you are at the car wash, and you're a little low on this particular day for your appointments. Let's say you want to go out and make five outside appointments. There are a couple ways you can do it. I recommend going to one of the businesses that you are working with. If you are at the car wash, go out there while these cars are coming through.

> "Hi, I'm Paul from the Fitness Center and we are working with the car wash. I have five gift certificates for $100 off enrollment. These certificates are for five people that get their car washed today. It's our way of helping promote the car wash. If you really think you will use this certificate I will put your name on it and we can set up a time for you to come in and see the club. When would you like to come in and pick it up? I have to take it back to my manager with your name and phone number on it because I am only allowed to give out five. That is how the club tracks the limited number of these certificates. If you are not really sure you will use this let me know because I don't want it to go to waste. What day is best for you to come down to the club and would that be before or after work?"

The other thing that you can use is the one month memberships:

> "Hey, I've got five one-week passes. Are you a member? Yes? Well is there someone that you would like this to go to? It could be anyone that you would enjoy exercising with. Your sister? Great. Do you have her name and number? I'll call her if you really think that she wants it. I'll go ahead and write her name down and take it to my manager. They will set up a time for her to come in and use her pass."

> "Hey, I've got five one-week passes. Are you a member? No? Great. Would you like to come in and try the club for a week? If you are really serious I have one 1 month membership I have to give out today. You get a personal training session, two free tans, and full use of the facility for a month. When would you like to come in and activate it?"

You just made an outside appointment. Outside appointments are very important, if you are low on your daily appointment quota. Each sales counselor should make at least six appointments daily. Every membership counselor should also have six appointments minimum every day. If you are halfway through the day and you are a general manager and see that some of your appointments are low or someone on your staff has low appointments send them out to get outside appointments. They can stand in a parking lot anywhere and do this: "Hey, my manager just sent me over. I've got five of these. Do you want one?" Of course, never hand them out. Get the person's name and put that on the gift. When the staff member brings back the names and numbers, the general manager should check them to make sure no cheating is going on. Call up the recipient of the gift:

> "Hi, Andi, this is Evan, the General Manager over at the Fitness Center. You just got one of the five one-month memberships that we were giving out today and I wanted to call you personally and say congratulations. I see that you are going to come in Tuesday at 1:00 p.m. to meet with Paul. I will also be here if you have any questions. We are looking forward to getting you set up."

As the GM, you have just confirmed that appointment. Calling not only holds your sales staff accountable, but the potential member thinks, "Wow, the GM just called me." It creates more value. And that is very important.

If you are a General Manager, there is no reason why all of your membership counselors cannot have six appointments. That is possible! You can do it, but you have to be disciplined to complete the daily checklists which you set up for your business. Look over their appointments, and if they have to make their appointments outside, send them out. That should only take an hour or so. Confirm a few of them to make sure they are not cheating, and go from there.

Chapter 10:
Corporate Sales

Corporate Sales involves enrolling large groups of people from businesses. Enrolling people this way takes a lot of people off the market that might otherwise enroll at a different fitness facility. It also enables people to enroll in a very easy, smooth way instead of having to come into your club as an individual member.

If a company enrolls their employees in your club, it enables them to invest in their employees and invest in your club. It creates a long-term dependable dues-base. In one two-year period, I enrolled several corporations in group memberships and not one company cancelled their membership. Once they start, it becomes very successful for the company. And you continue to receive new memberships.

Another benefit to corporate sales is that it targets a market of people who might not otherwise invest or set foot in a fitness center. And once a company gets started, it is infectious. People who work together notice someone building muscle, losing weight, or otherwise reaching their fitness goals. It creates positive synergy.

Some companies are what I call "fat" companies. This does not mean that people who work there are all overweight. It means that the food available there is high in fat. Some companies create positive peer pressure around food. Break rooms are filled with high-carbohydrate, high-fat foods such as cinnamon rolls, doughnuts or pastries. Soda machines or dessert snacks are provided by employees, and when workers are bored or stressed they can easily access foods high in fat. Workers often talk about their latest diets or plans to exercise. But at staffer's birthday parties, a large cake is served and workers who try to decline a piece of cake are often teased or mocked for not taking part in the party. "C'mon, eat it. What's up with you? Shelly made the cake, and it's really good." Food is simply a part of the company's culture, and it is hard for employees to resist the temptation to skip breakfast or lunch and eat the snacks in the break room or from the vending machines.

Corporate sales help companies change a culture of food into a culture of fitness. Picture this: break room junk food starts to slowly disappear, since many people who work out don't want to waste 30 minutes of hard work on one cinnamon roll. Guys start noticing Ben, who seems to be getting stronger. His chest and shoulders are starting to fill out his work uniform and he has to get pants with a smaller waist size that fit better. Guys start to want that for themselves. Gals start noticing Cynthia wearing new clothes to work; her old clothes do not fit her well any longer, and she feels ten years younger. Women start to want that for themselves.

The Bottom Line

Why should companies invest in corporate memberships for their employees? The bottom line is this: dollars and cents. Money! Companies that invest in wellness programs for their employees save hundreds, sometimes thousands and millions of dollars in health insurance costs. GMAC, which employs a comparatively large percentage of the United States work force, has a phenomenal wellness program in place for their employees because they save millions and millions of dollars. It is a proven fact that people that exercise on a regular basis are healthier. They do no call in sick as often, they are more productive, and they are not going to see the doctor constantly because they are not sick! It saves tons and tons of money. Furthermore, if people are in shape then their reaction time is often better, and they are often able to avoid more workplace accidents. Employees who are fit are less prone to have accidents on the job. Again, that creates more net income for the company.

Companies may care about creating a culture of fitness at their workplaces, but that may not be enough of a reason to do it. But when you are talking to corporate managers or human resource directors, the bottom line is that it will save them a lot of money.

Helping Their Retention Rate

Companies that have invested in bonus programs are proven to have a better retention rate for their employees. For example, if you have a restaurant with fifty servers and busers and bartenders, the turnover is pretty high. If they are paying $20 or so a month it is already being deducted out of their paycheck for a fitness membership that they are avidly using, there is a better chance they may stick around if another opportunity presents itself. They love that benefit.

How to Get Corporate Leads

Every single guest that comes into your facility will fill out a liability waiver when they come into the club. Simply put the *employer information* on your waiver. Approximately 95% of the people that walk into your facilities will be employed locally, within an hour's drive from your club. Those waivers are an awesome source of leads.

If you see thousands and thousands of guests over a period of years, then you will accumulate thousands and thousands of fitness profiles. These are an amazing source of leads. Sift through these profiles and call a human resources director.

> "Hi, this is Sandy from the Fitness Center. Jerry Wiltse is a member here and he paid retail rates on a membership. I'm calling to see if you are open to the possibility of starting a corporate membership program for your employees since some of your employees are already using our facility."

This is a really easy segue into a sales presentation. You are telling the truth—the employee paid the retail rate, and they are using your club. They are a member.

Another good way to get a source of corporate leads is if you are a member of your local Chamber of Commerce. Most clubs are. Utilize the chamber's directory which likely has hundreds or thousands of leads. And these leads will have the information that you need: the company's name, contact information, manger and owners' names, etc. Get the directory and utilize it over a period of months.

Yet another good way is to place a fishbowl at your front desk and have a business card drawing for a free personal training session. That alone could give you hundreds of leads in the course of a month.

Another more obvious way is to utilize the phone book! The phone book, of course, has pretty much every business in your area. This should be the last source that you use, since you will have hundreds or thousands of leads from the other sources listed above.

Whom to Contact

Now, whom should you contact at a business or corporation? You do not really want to talk to the owner—that is why owners hire Human Resources Directors. Those are the staff people who handle wellness programs or promotions.

I have learned through trial and error that if you get a hold of an owner or manager the first thing he or she is going to say is "no." They do not even want to think about it, and they aren't even open to it. Contacting the owner is not a very successful way to pursue it! Ask for the Human Resources Director. The best lead-in to your conversation is this:

> "Do you have any kind of a wellness program in place for your employees at this time?"

If the answer is no, follow up with this:

> "Well, are you open to the possibility to hearing about the Fitness Center? We have four locations and we have a lot of major companies in our region that have gotten started on our program, including . . ." and then list a few prominent companies which have signed up, to perk their interest. "All I really need from you is five minutes of your time to explain how it works. The best thing about the program is that it does not cost you any money."

Now, if they have not listened up to that point, guess what? They are listening now. A lot of times the man or woman will respond, "Wait a minute, it doesn't cost us anything?"

> "It doesn't cost you anything, and everybody gets in at a ridiculously low rate. Everybody wins."

The response that you will get is usually positive. Make an appointment!

The best time of the day to call on corporate leads is when the business is open! That's a *huge benefit* over a lead box when you are calling people and no one is home and you have to leave messages. On some days, your counselors will call lead box leads, where no one is home or screening their calls and your entire staff might make 100 phone calls and not a single person is home to answer! Instead, you can train your staff to make corporate lead calls. You will get a lot of progress during normal business hours, and the balance of the evening can be used for lead box calls or referrals when most people are home from work. Spreading out your contacts like this during the day balances out the day and makes a lot of sense.

Sample Corporate Sales Demonstration

Read the following demonstration of a corporate sales demonstration. Note the words in italics which help make the close and point a potential customer toward their bottom line:

> "Hey Barbara, thanks for seeing me. Here's my business card. If I could get one from you, that would be great. Thank you very much. I want to cover everything on the program with you just like we talked on the phone.

> "It is really quite simple. This is how it works. First of all, once you are on the program all of your employees and yourself have access to all of our locations. We have 7 locations in the greater metropolitan area as well as an eighth location in the next city an hour away. Three of our locations are open 24 hours a day. So that gets rid of the excuse of, "Gee, I don't have time to work out," which is probably the biggest excuse that we hear in the facilities.

> "The second page in our packet just tells you some of the reasons why companies invest in wellness programs. Most HR directors that I talk to are pretty aware of the reasons and the benefits. There's the reason of fitness, that everybody is going to look better and feel better. But the most common reason is dollars and cents. Companies invest in wellness programs because it's been proven over and over again that they save thousands and sometimes millions of dollars in health insurance costs. People that exercise regularly do not get sick as often, visit the doctor fewer times per year, and get hurt less often. That's been a proven fact time and time again. GMAC employs a comparatively large percentage of the United States population and they have a phenomenal wellness program because it saves them millions and millions of dollars in health insurance costs.

> "The next section reviews the rates of our membership. First, the retail rate. If you were walking into the club off of the street as a perspective member the presentation would go over the enrollment fee, the processing fee, and the monthly fee for membership, which is around $40 currently. With different marketing specials and advertising we sometimes discount the enrollment fee, but typically a new member pays some sort of an enrollment fee up front. The benefits are these: all access, two hours with a certified personal trainer. A member can add family members to their membership plan for a processing fee and less money per month, usually around $20.

For a couple to belong to our clubs, the monthly dues are about $60 per month, one dollar per day, per person. That is the retail rate.

"I would like to show you a couple of programs that we offer. First, here is a list of the companies in our region which have gotten started with us. A local hospital is on the program, as well as the employees of the city—the entire municipal workforce has joined so those employees have the option to join up through their organization. We also have an industrial company which had 250 of their employees join. You don't have to have many employees for the program—I'll explain the options to you.

"The Bronze Program is for companies that have between 50-99 employees. The company pays a $500 enrollment fee and that covers everyone who joins. So employees are able to walk in to a club, pay their $40 and start working out. It's a great program for them, and they are able to get in and get started for practically nothing.

"The second program is called the Gold Program. When companies are looking at both options, most of them go for the gold because they want their employees to have a little bit of an edge rate-wise over everybody else who is working out in the club. The initial investment is $1,000, which is a write-off, and a drop in the bucket compared to what some companies spend on Christmas parties. So you invest $1000, which covers all enrollment and processing fees and lowers the monthly dues to $30, and family add-ons are half of that.

"The Platinum Membership is very popular with companies. The thing about the first two options is that you are ultimately crossing your fingers and hoping that your workforce uses the memberships. There is no guarantee that after you spend $1000 that your employees will join up, or that they will use the facility. The Platinum Program is popular, and this is how it works: it is set up on a payroll deduction program. Rather than your employees going into the clubs and paying their membership dues off of their own checking account, debit card or savings account, it is automatically deducted off of their paycheck through your company. The minimum is 25 employees. If you can get 25 people to say, "Yes I want to exercise" it's only $19 per month. No up-front fees. No catch.

"The advantage of this is that a lot of companies have a handful of employees that cannot enroll because they do not have a checking account for whatever reason, or do not have a savings account, or simply aren't able to reap the benefits of working out in a fitness center. With this program, that is not an issue. And many people will not even miss $20. Most companies pay their employees twice per month, so a worker would be splitting the $20 in half. So if they are not going to really miss it. Plus, they do not have to go through the process of walking into a fitness center, taking the tour, hearing the presentation and giving them their account information. They get a certificate from their employer, they take their certificate to the club and they get their membership. Period. For $20 a month you will have people that maybe never even thought of joining a fitness center jump on the bandwagon because the rate is so inexpensive.

"If you can get 25 employees, this is the way it works. Step one is getting the word out to your staff. Use e-mail, flyers, a group meeting, or whatever you prefer. Get a head count of people who want to do it. What works most effectively is the attitude and enthusiasm of the HR director. If you are behind it 100%, they are going to be behind it. If you simply say, "Oh, this is going to be available," then you probably will not get a reaction. Rather, say this: "Hey, this is going to be a fantastic program. This is a great opportunity, and I encourage everyone to get started on the program. I'm getting started on the program." Saying that will get a lot more people following you. I will leave a sample payroll deduction form for you if you do not have one already. Get a head count, and give your staff a date to respond by. Try to create some urgency so they will get back to you. Once you have all of the payroll deduction forms signed and returned to you, call me with the total of primary members and add-ons. I will get the exact number of certificates you will need. I'll bring the certificates to you, you give me the check, and everybody is happy. Sound good? Yes? Great. Welcome to the program."

Chapter 11:
Amenities

In this chapter I would like to discuss two types of health club amenities. The first type brings in *direct* income for the health club business and the second brings in *indirect income.*

Direct Income

Direct income-generating amenities include personal training, tanning, pro shops, and juice bars. Amenities generating direct income are amenities that guests pay for over and above their membership fees. Of course, amenities generating direct income also *affect* indirect income. Income generating services influence indirect income by influencing the decision making process of guests.

Amenities play a big role in whether a guest becomes a member of a health club. A service that generates direct income (or a profit center as they are often called) might not actually break even. That does not necessarily mean the service should not be provided. A day care service might not break even in a health club but it might increase sales at the juice bar making it more profitable. Many people might choose one club over another because of a daycare service.

Indirect Income

Amenities generating indirect income are those that members do not pay for directly. These could be such things as group fitness, swimming pools, steam rooms, saunas, climbing walls, or baby sitting. Decisions on what services to provide members that are included in their memberships fees will affect membership sales. This would even include the club hours of operation!

One theory is to provide everything ever offered by a club including being open 24 hours a day. The theory is that this eliminates all objections a guest may have for becoming a member. I will not argue with this theory. However I will remind health club owners and operators that the purpose of operating a health club or any other business is to make and maximize profit. That being said, every decision on amenities and services offered should be made with the goal of maximizing profit. Every thing under the sun might be offered in a health club that ultimately is not profitable. As a matter of fact, it could lose a lot of money because it is offering more than the market is willing to pay for.

Hours of Operation

There are as many variables involved in determining what to provide in a health club as there are in determining pricing. Let's use the hours of operation as an example. If a club operator chooses to be open 24 hours a day, that decision should be judged by the revenue it generates, not by how many members use or will use the club at 3:00 a.m. The key question instead is this: *how many members will join* because they can use the club at

3:00 a.m.? That is the key question. Being open 24 hours a day may be a deciding factor on whether a guest joins your club or the one down the road even though that guest will never use the club at 3:00 a.m. The bottom line is this: if being open 24 hours a day brings in more income that the expense associated with it, then it is a smart move.

Of course, determining its profitability is very difficult. If an operator does a poll in the club asking members if a steam room should be added, the members will vote overwhelmingly to put in a steam room. But that does not mean it would be profitable to add a steam room. Everyone wants a steam room, but very few will ever use it. If the steam room increases profit it should be added.

We had a climbing wall in one of our clubs. Many people joined because they thought it was cool, but most of those people never used it. The choice to put in a climbing wall was a good one. It has paid for itself many times over. We also put in a golf simulator in one of our other clubs. This was a bad choice. This machine is a lot of fun but it cost us nothing but money and I don't think more than three people joined our club because we had it. No one seems willing to pay to use it.

Group Fitness

Group fitness is an amenity that most clubs offer. It is very important to hire an experienced, knowledgeable and dedicated Group Fitness Director. A dedicated director can advise on the rapidly changing fads and trends in the group fitness arena. The decisions to be made in this area are also infinite. How many classes should be offered? What and when should they be? How much should be paid to instructors? Should instructors be allowed to teach at other facilities? All these decisions should be based on the business environment, the growth of the community and potential future competition.

Day Care

The laws in each state differ for daycare and babysitting. Running a daycare out of a health club can be very expensive, but higher fees can be charged for providing the service. Babysitting is less expensive to operate but parents are usually required to be in the facility when their children are dropped off. There are many judgment calls to be made here also. It is most important to remember that every decision should be based on the goal of maximizing profit. Some facilities offer free babysitting. If free babysitting increases membership volume above the cost of providing babysitting, it is wise to offer free babysitting. Some cities allow clubs to charge for babysitting. If this is the case, then some of the cost of babysitting can be covered by charging for the service.   A club without any services for children might gross less but the *profit* might be more. Remember, maximizing profit is the goal.

Selling Trainer Services

Trainer services are a great way to build confidence in your members, help them reach their fitness goals, and help your bottom line. For more in-depth information on selling services, see Section II of this book on sales. What follows is some specific information which will help you sell your trainer services at your club.

The Questions to Ask

Start with questions. Try to find out what your member is looking for and tell them how trainer services will help them reach their goals:

1. Establish Goals – what are you looking for? What do you want to look like? Do you want to feel better? Look better? Try not to focus on their weight but rather on their overall goals.

2. Establish Stress Levels – on a scale of 1-10, how stressed are you right now?

3. Establish Endurance – about how long would it take you to run a mile?

4. Establish Permanence – are you looking for permanent results? You might say, "Some people are not serious about change, so it's great that you are serious enough to be talking with me about this."

5. Establish Importance – why is this important to you? Why are you interested in doing this now?

Results in Less Time with Less Effort

When you sell trainer services, sell a *permanent results program.* What a potential customer of training services is wanting is *the quickest results possible in the shortest period of time with the least amount of effort* on their part.

Trainer services create a program to get members from point A (where they are currently) to point B while decreasing their body fat percentage. American culture is fixated on the scale – how many pounds we weigh, how many pounds we want to lose. Trainer services, in contrast, lower body fat percentage while focusing on five different factors:

1. Proper Meal Planning
   When you sell your services, make sure people understand that they will not have to starve themselves or eat foods they cannot stand to eat. Instead, meal planning incorporates their lifestyle and foods they enjoy into and overall plan which is realistic and helps them achieve their goals. It will be a meal plan they can agree to follow! And it is a plan that the trainer will hold them accountable to. In fact, 75% of the results someone is looking for are found in what he or she is or is not eating!

2. Proper Cardiovascular Training
   When you sell trainer services, be sure to explain the difference between vigorous exercise and exercise which sustains a target heart rate. Working with a trainer will help a member sustain their target heart rate and metabolize, or burn, the fat they want to burn without burning muscle. It is also important to vary your cardio workouts from time to time, and trainers will help you do this appropriately without injuring yourself or aggravating previous injuries.

3. Proper supplementation
   When you sell trainer services, explain what proper supplementation is, and how

much cheaper it is to supplement your diet than it is to eat perfectly all of the time. If your trainers do not receive commission on the supplements and meal replacements that you sell at your club, it will set their customers at ease about supplementing their diet with the products that you sell at your club.

4. How to Use the Equipment Properly
    When you sell trainer services, make sure the member knows that a trainer will help determine which machines are best for their needs, and how to work out in such a way as to build muscle and not stress their joints. Members need to avoid injuries when they work out, and if they go out alone and uneducated they could hurt themselves or hurt their chances of reaching their goals. Trainers will help them find the path to get them the results they are looking for as quickly as possible.

5. Accountability with the Same Trainer
    When you sell trainer services, make sure the member understands that they will be working with the same person throughout their program. This trainer will hold them accountable along the way and help them to reach their goals in the shortest possible amount of time.

Basic Principles of Sales

Show success stories – build a notebook full of satisfied customers with before/after photos and testimonies of how they reached their goals

Emphasize fat loss over weight loss – a member might weight a few pounds more but still need smaller clothes.

Show a meal plan example – this will help a potential customer see that the food they will be eating on their meal plan will be realistic. Meal plans will always be geared toward their lifestyle.

Offer a variety of packages – 4 sessions, 8 sessions, 12 sessions and 16 sessions.

Discuss the Disadvantages of Going It Alone – if you try training on your own, you risk the chance of losing your motivation and not coming back to the facility as often. Working with a trainer gives you the opportunity to lose 1% of body fat per week, seeing a visual difference in your appearance in 4-5 weeks, and makes you more likely to stick with the program and get the results you are looking for.

The Bottom Line

When it comes to amenities, try to keep the bottom line clear. It will be easy to be distracted by your competition or by all the bells and whistles which are at your disposal. But grossing more money while profiting less money can result if you are not carefully evaluating your amenity options and making wise choices as to what to include in you club.

Chapter 12:
Effective Front Desk

Your front desk is the first impression that someone gets once they open the door to your club. The appearance of the outside of your club is important – that is truly the first impression. But it doesn't matter how attractive the facility is on the outside; if someone opens the door and experiences a poorly managed front desk, every positive impression they had before they opened the door is *gone in a flash.*

Hello and Goodbye

It is very important for people entering and leaving your clubs to be greeted. Think of it as "Hi and Bye."

You want to make sure that you have staff at your front desk who greet everyone entering your club and say "goodbye" to everyone leaving. This makes people feel good about coming into your club. For most people, it is the most difficult thing they do through the course of a day to carve out the time and actually come in and work out. So to see a friendly face behind the front desk saying "hello" to them makes it that much easier for them. And saying "goodbye" to them gives your club a more personal feel, which strengthens your business and helps reduce cancellations in the long run.

Answering the Phone

Phone etiquette is also very important. You would be surprised by how many people do not know how to speak on the phone properly. Answer your phones this way: "Thank you for calling the Fitness Center, how may we help you?" This kind of phone etiquette is very important because your callers could easily be potential members calling for more information about your club. If the person at the front desk answering the phone sounds friendly it will communicate that you have a friendly club, which is very important.

Fielding Questions

Another important role at the front desk is handling telephone inquiries. This is an area where the front desk and your sales department will work hand in hand. A telephone inquiry could be any number of questions such as questions about your rates or about your hours of operation. Train your front desk to give basic information and try to refer to a sales counselor as quickly as possible. Your sales staff will have the most knowledge about what type of specials are running, so you need to think of a telephone inquiry as *the beginning of the sales process* rather than as a problem to solve.

Guests With No Appointment

I intentionally refer to people as guests, because when someone walks into your club for information, they are your guest and should be treated accordingly. Do not use the terms "ma'am" or "sir" or "customer," but use the term guest, because that is what they are.

The way to handle a guest without an appointment is with the utmost respect. For some people it is a big step to come into a health club and it can be a bit intimidating. You want your front desk staff to be friendly, you want them to be encouraging, and more than anything you want them to be thorough. Get as much information about that person as you can, and then you want to get that person to talk to one of your sales associates for a tour of your club.

Introducing the Fitness Profile

Now, some clubs use a fitness profile; some do not. A fitness profile is an effective tool in finding out exactly what the fitness goals of your guest are. There are many different types of profiles. A solid profile would include information about eating habits, how much weight they would like to lose, how much muscle they hope to add, and what hours they can work out. With the profile, you want to get as much information as possible. Of course, some people are not comfortable in filling out the profile. One of the best ways to ease their concerns is to let them know that you are just trying to find out how best you can serve them in your club.

A Guest With An Appointment

The last critical role of your front desk is welcoming guests who have an appointment. Typically, your front desk staff will be expecting the person to come in, and this is another area where it is critical for the front desk to work in tandem with your sales department. The front desk should know the names and times for the appointments. This way, the front desk can greet the potential member by name, tell them they were expected, and then contact the sales rep to let them know that their appointment has arrived. You want your guest to be as comfortable as possible. The more professional the process becomes when a guest comes in for a scheduled appointment, the more likely a guest is to join. People want to join a club that has its act together.

As you know, the front desk can be a very busy place. There are guests checking in, there are members checking in, and often people are making purchases. One of the best ways that we keep everything straight is to have a Front Desk Log. This log is a spreadsheet with a long piece of paper that records all front desk activity: guests who have signed up for membership, items purchased, appointments that have arrived, and anything to do with the front desk operation. Even if you have a cash register or computer system which tracks purchases, I have found that a front desk log is the most effective way to quickly track things which have occurred throughout the day. It's a great way to keep your front desk organized and it even helps you prevent theft in your club.

It is likely that you have or will have several products that you sell which are out for people to see. Some of these products will be under lock and key, but others may be out in the open so members can see them and read labels and find out more information.

Inventory is a task which should be done by your staff several times a day. Doing this routinely will prevent theft and protect your bottom line. There are two primary reasons for this: first, it helps track your products so you can tell if something is missing. That way, if something is missing, the club knows about it. Secondly, you want your members to see that you are *paying attention* to the products that are out in the open. They need to know that they work out at a club that does not tolerate theft.

Always try to check your inventory against the front desk log. This way, you know if items were purchased or if they have gone missing. Do not be known as a club that tolerates theft or disorganization. Instead, utilize your front desk as a hub of your organization which not only works in tandem with your sales department but also your inventory control systems.

Chapter 13:
Keeping Customers Happy:
Basic Maintenance, Club Appearance and
Saving Cancellations

Saving Cancellations

Cancellations are a part of any health club organization. You will not be able to prevent everyone from canceling their membership. People leave a club for a variety of reasons, some of which you have no control over.

Your goal, though, should be to *minimize cancellations*. It will not do you any good to sign up 100 new members if 100 of them cancel their membership. What follows are some principles to keep in mind as you strive to keep your club looking sharp while minimizing cancellations.

The Customer Service Factor

Customer service has a critical role in minimizing cancellations. Often the most common complaint someone has who cancels their membership is that the club is not *kept clean*. Customer service staff need to work hard to make sure the day to day operation runs smoothly and that everything is clean and in order:

Your club is clean.
Your front desk is friendly.
Your bathrooms have adequate soap and paper products.
You are doing what you can to minimize complaints.
You are doing what you can to make members happy.

Again, checklists are critical to this operation. Using a customer service checklist properly will prevent sloppy work and minimize the kind of complaints which can lead to cancellations. Make sure your checklist is tailored to your club, whether you have a spa, a dry sauna, a steam room or all three. Also, make sure your checklist is constantly revised to highlight important issues which you may need to keep in front of you.

Maintenance and Club Appearance

Cleanliness of the club is a no-brainer – it's very important, and is the number one answer people give when asked why they are canceling their memberships.

The struggle is this: everyone has a different standard of what is clean. Should your club be as clean as a surgeon's operating room? No, of course not. But it should be as clean as someone wants their home to be, and if you have dirt, grime, trash and broken equipment everywhere, you will lose members right and left.

Everyone's Job

You should stress throughout the company that everyone takes part in the cleanliness of the club. Start with the outside. It's the first impression that everyone gets of your club when driving into your parking lot. Is your club well-landscaped? Is there garbage blowing around? Excessive dirt? Make sure the outside of your club is clean!

The locker room is another critical piece of the cleanliness factor. Imagine your bathroom at home being clean and spotless. Then imagine 600 people using it during the course of the day. What would it look like?

Make sure your locker room smells clean, that you use disinfectants and deodorizers, that the floors are mopped and that the lockers and clean and wiped down regularly. Make sure the sinks are clean, that paper is off the floor, and that your bathroom is adequately socked with soaps and paper products.

Equipment Maintenance

How quickly do you take care of broken equipment? Broken equipment is commonplace on a gym floor. With as many people as you have using equipment, it will wear out from time to time. The key question is, how quickly will you respond?

Keep a log and record all necessary maintenance. Report it quickly, so it gets taken care of quickly. Sometimes equipment will have to be down for awhile because parts have to be ordered. If this is the case, let your members know that parts are on order and that it will be repaired on a date when the parts are expected to arrive. Keeping members informed gives them a nice feeling that you care about them and that you have your act together.

The Sales Department Factor

Your customer service staff needs to be working hard to make sure complaints are minimized and that cancellations are minimized. But once a member decides that they want to cancel their membership, your sales department is critical to saving cancellations.

Many times a member will cancel because the club is not clean or because they are just not using their membership. Train your sales counselors to talk people through their hesitation, and if necessary offer personal training, free tanning, or other services to help encourage the member to stay. If you find out the real reason they are canceling, you will have a good chance of saving the cancellation by helping them get motivated and revitalized about the club.

Set Guidelines

Make sure your sales department knows exactly what they can and cannot offer a member to stay. Incentives may include personal training, free tanning or other fee services that you offer. That kind of clarity will help them serve the member in the best possible way without crossing any lines that their supervisor does not want them to cross.

The very last step in saving a cancellation is to offer to freeze their account. This should only be a last ditch effort to save the cancellation, but it does save the member the costs of signing up again. Usually members are grateful for this service, particularly if they are going to be out of town for an extended period or of if they will be otherwise unable to work out because of a season-of-life issue which will last several months.

Collections and Delinquencies

Dealing with collections and delinquencies is obviously unpleasant, but they are a necessary thing to do. You must work them, and pursue collections aggressively and fairly. It's an everyday part of what health clubs do.

Make sure that you have a program that runs a series of reports on which accounts are delinquent so that your staff can work those accounts.

Here are the steps you should take on an account that is delinquent:

1. Call the accounts. Find out the problem, try to set them at ease. It might have been a misunderstanding, and the member might not yet know there was even a problem at all.

2. Send a letter. Inform the member that they have a problem with their billing cycle. Make sure they are free to call you to get the problem taken care of. Sending a letter is a courtesy and again, the member may not be aware of the problem.

3. Use a collection agency. Sometimes there will be differences between you and the member which are irreparable. He or she does not care and they are not going to pay the money that they agreed to pay. Develop a relationship with a collection agency and make sure they have guidelines on what they can do with your accounts.

When you use a collection agency, do not feel guilty about doing it. It is the same way with the telephone company or with utilities. If you agree to pay them money and you default, it is their right to collect from you.

Remember, your goal with collections and delinquencies is to *get the member in good standing.* Set them up on payment plans, and accept partial payments if you need to. Do what you can to make members happy, and use collection agencies when the situation is irreparable.

Also remember to *keep yourself organized.* Use a log, and make detailed notes on calls so you know exactly what has been done on that account. Doing this helps you keep track of every individual account, and will help your staff when they call up an account to check the status and steps that have already been taken by your club.

Synergy

Teamwork is the key to success in your club: the synergy of your front desk, sales department and customer service department can come together to keep your club looking great and keep your members long-term.

Chapter 14:
Building Your Business

Health club businesses require multiple products and services in order to operate. Billing companies, cleaning services, wholesale products, payroll services and financial instruments are just some of the needs that need to be met.

Often a business can maximize its production and profitability by outsourcing, but not always and not in every area. The number of clubs in a chain and the economy of scale can help determine what should be *outsourced* and what should be kept *in house*.

Cleaning Services

It is not wise to hire a middle man for cleaning in the health club business. What I mean by a middle man is a cleaning company that hires low wage employees to clean a health club. In a period of ten years I have fired more cleaning companies than I can count. Most of them lasted about three months. The first week they do a great job because the owner or supervisor shows up with the night crew. Once the owner of supervisor moves on to the next customer, the night crew looks for a place to sleep or get in a quick work out. If the cleaning company you hire does not have employees, the problem of unsatisfactory work will not occur! What I mean is that the owner of the company does the work him or herself. The cost for cleaning is a lot lower also because the owner is not a middle man if there are no employees.

Ending the Cycle of Nonperformance

The cleanliness of the club is the responsibility of the operation manager in our system. This manager is in the club every day and checks for cleanliness. When the club is not up to par the manager typically calls the cleaning company or the middle man. The middle man calls the cleaning employees to motivate them but typically nothing happens. The middle man gives the manager lip service for about three month which is when the middle man or cleaning company gets fired.

Why not just have the manager call the cleaning employees directly? One great idea is this: why not set up your own cleaning company and give ownership of it to many of your key employees? Our clubs had never been cleaner and our employees had their own business. Structuring business this way is tremendous for employee retention and helps to build a future for our employees. This way, the managers hire and pay the employees in their own cleaning company. They monitor the staffs they have hired much better, because it is their responsibility to make sure the clubs are clean. They don't want their own cleaning company to be fired!

A Lesson in Micro-Economics

Over a period of time in the health club business I started to see that operating multiple facilities created a micro-economy. If you have more than one club, the size of your budget and your economy of scale will eventually be large enough to support many small businesses. Many products and services supplied to our health clubs are provided by businesses we had created. One new business we created is a t-shirt company. We can sell t-shirts to ourselves and to other companies at a lower price because our economy of scale gives us a lower overhead. We can buy and screen print t-shirts at a lower price than competitors because our t-shirt company doesn't have a rent payment or payroll. This was the same principle at play with the supply company we created.

If a good imagination is used, great businesses and income can be created using multiple health clubs and utilizing your own economy. Be creative!

Chapter 15:
Epilogue

There are as many strategies and philosophies in the health club business as there are cities in America. Many of these strategies are very effective. One strategy might be just as good as another, but one thing is for sure, most health clubs can do better. I would bet 99 out of 100 health clubs could be operated better and that includes my clubs.

This book will help the health club operators that are hungry to improve to get better at what they do. Many of the people that will read this book are far more knowledgeable than I am on this subject, but everyone in the industry that reads this book will gain something or get a fresh idea that was stimulated by something in this book. At the very least operators will be reminded of some basics that they are not applying as well as they should be.

If anything is gained from this book it should be to create a system and have the discipline to follow it. That system should also be able to change with time. Every business must change or it will die. Just because something worked yesterday does not mean it will work today or tomorrow—especially in today's rapidly changing technological environment.

For More Information

For more information on the online consulting services and products provided by Steve and his associates, call 800-507-6378 or email steve@healthclubmanagers.com or steve@worldgymnevada.com. The website is http://www.healthclubmanagers.com/

CPSIA information can be obtained at www.ICGtesting.com
Printed in the USA
LVOW031238210612

287086LV00005B/1/A